RELUCTANT PARTICIPANTS

ANIMALS AND THE AMERICAN CIVIL WAR

CHARLES P. POLAND JR.
Foreword by **LYNETTE P. HARVEY**

Copyright 2024

All rights reserved. This book or any portion thereof may not be reproduced or used in any manner whatsoever without the express written permission of the publisher except for the use of brief quotations in a book review.

ISBN: 979-8-35098-007-3 (softcover)
ISBN: 979-8-31780-077-2 (hardcover)
ISBN: 979-8-35098-008-0 (eBook)

To my talented grandsons, Kirby, Brady, Christopher, Preston, and Jackson, who have brought joy and pride to our family.

CONTENTS

Foreword by Lynette P. Harvey 1

Acknowledgments 3

Introduction 4

1. The Long History of War Animals 7

2. Recruiting the Civil War's Most Significant Animals 25

3. Training, Deployment, and Weaponry 50

4. Equine Celebrities 68

5. A Mind of Their Own 84

6. The Bond Between Man and Beast 94

7. The Tormentors 108

8. Hunger Trumps Affection 122

9. Animals As Military Targets 138

10. Companions in Misery 151

Bibliographical Comment 183

Index 187

FOREWORD
BY LYNETTE P. HARVEY

Since the beginning of mankind, there has always been a relationship between man and animals. As outlined in subsequent chapters of this book, animals were also very common in battle, from the initial use of horses in combat to the later refinement of the use of horses in cavalry divisions in the armed services. The field of Human-Animal Interaction (HAI) was born through these documented interactions between man and animals.

Horses and dogs are two species that predominate our histoy of HAI. The use of early service animals were used in battle for cavalry; mules were used for the transportation of goods and equipment; and dogs were used for many tasks, such as assisting in finding enemy platoons and serving as guards for prisoners of war during the Civil War.

Early findings of what we now know as therapy dogs or emotional support animals were found in the Civil War era. Animals served as mascots for the company they represented. Many dogs and horses not only served as work animals, but they provide companionship and comfort for many soldiers as much-needed morale boosters-a nice diversion from the drudgery of soldiers' lives.

The well-established bond we know exists between man and animal has been studied and analyzed in many aspects of HAI. This concept was historically demonstrated in how dogs would guard the bodies of their fallen owners during the Civil War. Of Course horse and cavalry soldiers were inseparable and worked tirelessly together as a working cog in the war machine. Animals were no exception to the cruelty of wartime; many animals suffered from disease, starvation, and lack of resources, as did their accompanying humans, which created an animal-to-man brotherhood of unspoken loyalty and belongingness.

It is through these initial beginnings of the relationship of man and beast that transformed HAI into what it is today. There is a plethora of documented benefits that animals provide to modern man. A specially trained service dog can now sense when their owner is about to have a seizure and alert this person before it occurs. The use of equine therapy has been monumental for veterans suffering from PTSD and for children with cerebral palsy. There are even documented cases of therapy goats visiting assisted living facilities, which increase residents' cognition and quality of life.

The personal relationship between pets and humans is even stronger today. It is common for pets to sleep with their owner or for a human to bring their dog when traveling. We owe these strengthened relationships to many of the early beginnings of the interaction of man and animal in the American Civil War.

— Lynette P. Harvey

Tennessee Technological University

ACKNOWLEDGMENTS

An author depends on the support of people, libraries, and archives, not the least of which is the moral support of my family, especially my wife, Betty. I am grateful for their moral support. My son-in-law, Paul McMahon, has provided valued and appreciated assistance in solving computer issues, as has my grandson, Kirby McMahon. Although we are on different topics, Dr. William Kinsella, Jr. has encouraged and stimulated discussions about his and my research. Charles Harrell has provided material for this book and much-appreciated encouragement. Fred Pitman has also graciously provided information. To Dr. Lynette Harvey, an academic scholar whose expertise includes the relationship between canines and the elderly, I am grateful for her extensive help. I also greatly thank Chanel Mullins for her cheerful and expert editing.

INTRODUCTION

The history of war animals is intertwined with that of humans, who determined their role in war, but the problems they faced and suffered, including hunger, disease, pain, and death, were similar. The story of animals used in wars is lengthy, surprisingly diverse, and sometimes bazaar. The most consistently used war animal was the horse. Modern technology during the 20th century dramatically diminished the vital roles of the horse and mule. Dogs have a long war history, but their role has continued and expanded, unlike the horse and mule. Four animals: horses, mules, cattle, and dogs were vital in the American Civil War from 1861 to 1865. The dominant animals used in the American Civil War were horses, which were critical for travel, communication, movement of supplies, and combat. Mules and occasionally oxen were used as draft animals, cattle were used for food, and hogs, sheep, and chickens were also necessary for sustenance. Animals also include insects. They, too, are members of the animal classification, having diverged from mammals and other animals long ago.

War interrupts not only civilian life but also wildlife. Birds, rabbits, and deer panicked, and birds flew disorganized in every direction when their environment erupted with the thunderous noise of gunfire and men swarming over the land. Lice, fleas, and ticks attached themselves to soldiers, tormenting them; bees stung them. Snakes occasionally frightened them.

Animals did not become involved in the war by choice. During peacetime or war, they are at the mercy of humans. Man dragged them as minions under his will into war. Many considered animals as living property to be used however they saw fit. Their treatment varied from brutality to caring. Some think animals are dumb and devoid of feelings, and their abuse is of no concern, failing to trigger any human remorse or empathy. The harsh contrast in the treatment of canines continued in the Civil War between being adored and exterminated. Yet, to many, their relationship with animals, especially the horse and dog, went beyond dependence to forming a close bond, a bond fostered in part by their reliance upon the other. However, their relationship became more than a partnership in which the animals did as ordered, and the owner provided the proper care. It became a relationship of affection and concern for each other.

Some feel that the study of animals should be part of environmental history. However, the animal rights organizations that started during the Civil War era ignited the history of animals. They decried the abuse of animals, including using them as war animals, and pointed out that animals were sentient creatures capable of sensing and feeling.

Soldiers found a break from the monotony of camp life and amusement in a pet, especially a dog. During the Civil War, some men took their dogs with them when they joined the army as companions from home. In addition to dogs, animals like cats, birds, goats, and unlikely creatures became mascots.

We do not know what exactly animals think, but their behavior gives us some indication. It frequently was one of protest. A kicking horse or mule was just one way of showing their disgruntledness. They suffered along with soldiers the lack of food, fatigue, disease, pain from wounds, and death. War significantly reduced their numbers, which surpassed that of humans.

There are over 60,000 books on the Civil War, and presses continue to churn out more each month. Still, the story of animals and the Civil War has been ignored, with only a scattering of works on famous horses until the last two decades. Naturally, most Civil War histories are about people and their relationship to war, but it is incomplete without including animals. One-and-a-half million horses died during the war. Although they played a secondary role to the humans who controlled them, war animals played a vital role and paid a heavy price in the war that changed America.

Reluctant Participants examines the value of animals as a resource in the Civil War, the impact of war upon them, and their relationship with humans.

CHAPTER 1

THE LONG HISTORY OF WAR ANIMALS

Men were not the only participants in the war. To gain a winning edge, he used animals as a combat resource. Numerous types of animals were used; many led to success on the battlefield, while others were less productive.

KEY WAR ANIMALS IN HISTORY

Historically, the most crucial animal used for military purposes is the horse. This involved pulling and being ridden. Modern warfare has eliminated their combat role, but their history as war animals is over 5,000 years old.

Throughout history, the type and size of horses used in combat depended on the need for speed or power. Lightweight horses (800 to 1,000 pounds) were used by cavalry for speed. The middleweights (1,000 to 1,200 pounds) carried heavily armored knights, pulled heavy wagons, and occasional artillery. Heavyweight equines (1,500 to 2,000 pounds), the forerunners of the present-day draft animals, pulled heavy supply wagons and artillery and were calm in combat.

The average horse can carry about 30 percent of its body weight and pull more than it can carry. There were many variables for determining what type of horse to use, such as the size of the horse, the weight of what was being moved, and the condition of the road or land. The invention of the saddle, stirrup, and horse collars significantly increased the effectiveness of horses in battle and their use as draft animals. Early warfare in the ancient world involved horses pulling chariots. Improvements in wheels, axles, and weapons resulted in the chariots being used in the Bronze Age from China to Egypt. Gradually, the chariots were superseded by cavalry, fighting and riding horses in the ancient world. During the Middle Ages, armored knights and forces used the middleweight horse, prominent on the European continent, to combat the fierce mounted barbarians. The early modern period saw the shift from armored knights and heavy cavalry to unarmored light cavalry. During the Napoleonic Wars, horses weighing around 1,000 pounds were preferred. Mares and geldings that were five years old or older were selected over unruly stallions that were also five years old. A cavalry horse served ten to 12 years, barring injury or illness. Losses of 30 to 40 percent were typical in combat.

Extensive training was required whether a horse was pulling chariots, carrying an armored knight, or performing in the cavalry. The horse's instincts are to flee when it smells blood, hears a noise, or sees sudden movements, including those made by the rider using their weapons. Manuals were written from ancient to modern times on how to teach the equine to overcome skittish behavior during combat. Some training encouraged horses to kick and bite, making them into weapons.

During the early 16th century, the Spanish introduced horses to the indigenous people of the Americas, who soon became skilled at using them. Unlike the Continental Army, which made little use of cavalry during the American Revolution, the American Civil War saw cavalry hold "the most important and respected role it would ever hold in the American military."[1]

The cavalry was used extensively worldwide in the 1800s but waned at the beginning of the 20th century. The horse's role focused more on pulling or carrying supplies. During World War I, trench warfare, barbed wire, and the introduction of the tank in 1917 made cavalry impractical on the Western Front. The cavalry was more critical on the Eastern Front, with less trench warfare. Despite the declining importance of the horse in warfare, over 8,000,000 perished in World War I from harsh conditions at the front, disease, drowning in water, and battle casualties. The American army had a surplus of horses at the war's end, selling about half a million for work, especially to farmers. Unwanted horses were to be destroyed, and 61,000 were sold for food.[2]

During World War II, American cavalry use was minimal. Several countries, including Poland, Germany, the Soviet Union, and Britain (early in the war) used cavalry. But the role of the horse was shifting from combat to transport. Horses and mules were essential throughout the war for transporting material needed for combat. This was especially true for the Germans and Soviets. Germany was extremely short of motorized transport because her factories were required to produce tanks and planes. Eighty percent of Germany's transport was horsedrawn. The German army entered World War II with 514,000 horses and, by the end of the war, had grown to 2,700,000, depleting Europe of horses.[3] The Soviets used 3,500,000 horses. Sources vary on the fatality numbers of horses in the war.

---

[1] "Horses in Warfare," Wikipedia, https://en.wikipedia.org/wiki/Horses-in-warfare.
[2] "Horse Power in the First World War," https://www.nam.ac.uk/explore/horse-power.
[3] "Where did the Germans get so many horses for WW2?" https://www.quora.com.

Some contend that two million horses were killed during World War II, while others assert it was half that or three times higher. It is estimated that over half of the horses were killed by gunfire, a third from overwork, and the rest from disease and exposure, like the cold of Russia. At the start of the war, a horse had a life span of six months, but by the end, it was six weeks compared to those that lived on a farm, which could live 25 years.[4]

After World War II, horses disappeared from the battlefield. An exception was the use of horses by United States forces to liberate Afghanistan from the Taliban in 2001.[5]

Horses have been joined in supporting human warfare by two other equids: donkeys and mules. Donkeys and mules have been pack animals since antiquity, but mules have become more dominant for transport. They are unique creatures—the offspring of a male donkey (a jack) and a female horse (a mare).[6] Their stubbornness is outweighed by their strength, surefootedness, greater endurance than a horse, carrying heavy loads for longer distances, eating a third less than a horse for the same work, withstanding heat better, and being more disease-resistant. They often sensed an ambush before soldiers, indicated by their ears flaring out. Mules were used as pack animals, pulling baggage carts for Roman legions, and participated in ancient Greece Olympics in mule cart races. Throughout history, armies have used mules to transport supplies over mountain trails and remote areas. Their service continued through both the world wars and Afghanistan in 2001. During the second half of the

---

4 "Where did the Germans get so many horses for WW2?" https://www.quora.com/Where-did-the-Germans-get-so-many-horses-for -WW2?
5 "Horses in Warfare," Wikipedia, https://en.wikepedia.org/wiki/Horses-in-warfare.
6 "Mule," Wikipedia, https://en.wikipedia.org/wiki/mules. "The Virtues of Stubbornness Mules at War" https://www.defensemedianetwork.com/stories/t. The donkey and horse are different species. Mules vary in color and size, the latter determined by the largeness of the horse. The offspring of a male donkey and a female horse is a hinny. They are sometimes mistaken for a mule even though they are smaller with a donkey's body and a horse's limbs.

20th century, in industrial countries, the use of mules for farming and transport drastically declined due to tractors and trucks. Today, 3,500,000 donkeys and mules are butchered annually for meat worldwide, with China and Latin America being the primary consumers.[7]

The largest and strongest war animal is the elephant. Their primary use in combat was to charge and break through the enemy's ranks, creating fear and panic. Although difficult to control and not considered domesticable, elephants have been used in war from ancient times through World War II. They have been trained to move heavy loads and be ridden. They can carry 800 to 1,200 pounds and pull up to 8,000 pounds for 15 to 20 hours. The disadvantage of using elephants in combat is illustrated in the Battle of Zama in Africa (modern-day Tunisia) in 204-203 BC. The great Roman general Scipio Africanus countered an attack by the Carthaginian general Hannibal with 80 elephants by placing his legions into columns and had his men bang on their mess pots and shout. The loud noise frightened the elephants, causing their riders to lose control. Some giant creatures were channeled into the gaps between the Roman columns and killed. Others turned back and ran away, trampling Carthaginian soldiers. The invention of gunpowder caused the rapid decline of the use of elephants in battle. They could withstand musket fire but not cannons. Their size made them easy targets, so they were relegated to transport, including World War II. Both the Allies and Japan used elephants in locations where vehicles could not travel.[8]

---

[7] "Mule," Wikipedia, https://en.wikipedia.org/wiki/mules. "The Virtues of Stubbornness Mules at War," http://www.defensemedianetwork.com/stories/t.

[8] "Military Animals," Wikipedia (https:en;Wikipedia.org/wiki/military_animals); "Animals in War" https://www.thecollector.com/animals-used-in-war. Hannibal crossed the Alps with a few elephants in the Second Punic War, but only one survived. Elephants were used in Asia long before and after the fall of the Roman Empire. During the 16th century, the ruler of the Mughal Empire, Babur, had over 112,000 elephants, with 12,000 in military service.

A draft animal that has received limited historical attention despite being used for work since 4000 BC is the ox (also called oxen or bullock). Oxen are castrated male cattle, which makes them more docile and easier to handle. They have been used during war and peacetime to pull heavy loads. On farms, they were used for plowing. In England, they were used as draft animals and for beef. Their advantage over a horse is their strength and ability to pull heavier loads for longer. Their disadvantage is that they are slow. A yoke is placed around their necks next to the shoulder and attached to whatever they pull. They usually work in pairs, and hauling heavy loads over rugged terrain might require ten or more teams. Drivers often used a whip or stick to encourage their movement. Like horses and mules, oxen had to be taught to respond to commands. In North America, the standard commands for draft animals such as horses, mules, and oxen are: "back" to back up, "gee" to turn right, "get up" (also "giddyup") to go, "haw" to turn left, and "whoa" to stop. Usually, working oxen require shoes. Because their hooves are cloven, each hoof needs two shoes. Unlike horses, oxen have trouble standing on three feet, making them difficult to shod.[9]

Camels have been used in desert warfare as pack animals and cavalry throughout the Middle East's history. They require less water and withstand heat better than horses, making them better suited to survive in waterless and arid terrain than equines. The Romans, Napoleon, and other countries used camels in war in arid environments, and they were used in both world wars to transport food, water, ammunition, and other items needed by armed forces. India and Jordan still use camels for border patrol.

---

9   "Ox Wikipedia, (https://enwikipedia.org/wiki/Ox. In England, the ox is thrown to the ground, and the feet are tied to a strong wooden tripod until the process is completed. In Italy, the ox is lifted off the ground using heavy lumber, and the feet of the animals are tied to the structure.

The smell of a camel unnerved horses and made the camel an anti-cavalry weapon in the Battle of Thymbra in 547 BC. The Persian cavalry was outnumbered by the Lydian cavalry six to one. Cyrus the Great of Persia acted on information that horses shied away from camels and took his camels from his baggage train, forming a camel cavalry. The appearance and smell of camels panicked the horses of the Lydian cavalry, resulting in victory for Cyrus the Great.[10]

Of all the war animals, the dog and horse evoked the greatest affection from soldiers. Despite the canine's friendly side, as they are today used in therapy, they could be a vicious adversary to the enemy. Different breeds and sizes of dogs have been used for various purposes in warfare. Since the seventh century BC, their duties varied from attacking the enemy to serving as sentries, scouts, trackers, message carriers, mascots, sniffing out explosives, and service dogs. They were also used as mercy or casualty dogs to find wounded and dying on the battlefield. During ancient times, the Greeks, Romans, and other civilizations would use large mastiff-type breeds, some weighing 280 pounds, outfitted in armor and spiked collars to attack the enemy. Attila the Hun used large dogs in his campaigns. The Spanish used large dogs in the 1500s against Native Americans. During World War II, Americans gave their dogs to the military to be used as war dogs. About 20,000 dogs served with the American forces. They performed valued service in guarding posts, carrying messages, rescuing downed pilots, and leading troops through enemy territory. They executed similar service in Vietnam, where they were trained to hunt the Viet Cong in numerous tunnels. Approximately 5,000 dogs with 10,000 handlers were used in Vietnam. During this conflict, dogs are credited with saving 10,000 US service members.

---

10   "Camel Cavalry," Wikipedia, https://en.wikipedia.org/camel_cavalry. "Military Animals," Wikipedia, https:en.wikipedia.org/wiki/military_animals.

After World War II, dogs were returned to their former owners in the United States or adopted by their handlers. By contrast, the shortage of food for pets at the start of World War II caused the British to euthanize 750,000 domestic animals in one week, mainly dogs and cats. Similar harsh treatment befell dogs after the Vietnam War. They were "designated as expendable equipment" and euthanized or given to the Allied forces. Congressional legislation in 2000 finally allowed them to be adopted.[11]

Birds were also used as war animals. Homing pigeons were used to carry messages 3,000 years ago. Their ability to find their way home is believed to be based on a type of protein in birds' eyes. Several animals also have this. This gives them a sense (called magnetoreception) that allows them to detect magnetic fields and use it as a compass, directing them to the location they desire.[12]

Homing pigeons are domestic pigeons derived from the wild rock dove, which has a natural homing ability. They carry messages only one way: to their home. They had to be transported to another location to send a message back to their home.[13] During both world wars, planes carried them away from their home. Pigeons have been recorded flying over 1,000 miles. Their average flight speed for 600 miles, a moderate distance, is 60 miles an hour, which they can sustain while carrying a message wrapped around their leg. Ancient Rome used pigeons to send messages to their territory, Gaul. Even after the invention of the radio, they were used in wars in the 20th

---

11   Stanley Coren, *The Intelligence of Dogs* (New York: The Free Press, 1994), 138-139. "Dogs in Warfare," Wikipedia, https://en.wikipedia.org>wikiDogs_in."How many dogs have been killed in war? https://www.quora.com>How-many.war-dogs-have-b.
12   Cryptochrome (Cry4) is part of a class of proteins called cryptochromes in the bird's eye that enabled them to find their way home.
13   "Homing Pigeons," Wikipedia, https://en.wikipedia.org/wiki/Homing_pigeon. Homing pigeons have now been trained to fly both ways by placing food at a location away from their home. Homing pigeons are also called mail pigeons or messenger pigeons. They are frequently incorrectly called English Carrier pigeons, an ancient breed that lost their homing ability.

century. In World War II, the United Kingdom used approximately 250,000 homing pigeons. Later in the war, the danger increased for homing pigeons as the enemy shot them, killing and maiming many.

During World War I, one severely wounded pigeon lost an eye and foot but somehow delivered a critical message hanging from a ligament in its shattered leg, saving surrounded American soldiers. Another amazingly flew 52 missions unharmed.[14]

UNLIKELY WAR ANIMALS

Throughout history, man, during wars, has selected animals they believed could inflict harm upon the enemy. This led to selections that seemed bizarre. One example is the use of bees in ancient and modern wars. The Greeks successfully defended Themiscyra in 72 BC by putting bees down the tunnels the Romans dug underneath the city's walls. Three years later, Romans were again thwarted when defenders placed poisoned honey in beehives on the way to their city in modern Turkey. The honey sickened Roman soldiers and led to their defeat. German and British soldiers were recipients of angry, stinging bees during World War I. The Vietcong used bees against US soldiers, waiting until US patrols arrived and then setting off fireworks near a beehive, causing the angry bees to attack the Americans.[15]

Another insect used was the mosquito. The Germans in Italy during World War II flooded the Pontine Marshes south of Rome to create malaria among the Allied troops. They got sick, but it did not stop their advance.

---

[14] "War Pigeons," Wikipedia, https://en.wikipedia.org/wiki/Homing_pigeons. "Homing Pigeons," Wikipedia, pigeons. In races, homing pigeons have been known to fly 100 miles per hour. During World War II, 32 pigeons received the Dickin Medal for their gallantry in saving human lives.

[15] "Animals in War: 7 Examples of Animals Fighting in Human Conflict," https://www.thecollector.com/animals-used-in-War.

Scorpions were used by the Athenians in 198 BC when the Romans besieged their city, Hatra (now modern Iraq). The Athenians filled pots with dozens of scorpions and threw them down upon attacking Romans. This may have helped blunt the Roman attack, but the hot weather and illness among Roman soldiers ultimately ended their assault.

Another unsuccessful plan was to develop a moose cavalry to replace the horse. Moose had been used in Sweden to pull sleighs. The idea circulated in Europe was that the moose would frighten horses by scattering them without gunfire. There is information that the Soviets experimented in 1939–1940 by replacing the horse cavalry with moose but abandoned the idea. Moose did not take to being ridden; gunfire unsettled them, and they were more susceptible to disease than horses and were challenging to feed. They did not adjust to being fed fodder and restricted from grazing over a large area.[16]

Surprisingly, reindeer were important in World War II in the Arctic, where a vital supply route from the US to Russia crossed northern Norway. The Germans constantly threatened it. Reindeer carried many supplies over this country on the way to Russia. Naval historian Tim Francis contends that successfully using this supply route "might have been impossible without the help of some of Santa's friends."[17]

Felines are well known as comforting companions, mascots, and morale boosters for soldiers during war and for keeping the rodent population in check, especially on ships. Still, they are considered by many unlikely participants in combat. For more than 2,500 years, from Egypt and Persia to Europe in World War II, cats

---

16 "Moose Cavalry," Wikipedia, https://en.wikipedia.org/wiki/Moose_cavalry.
17 "In WWII, Reindeer Were Our Animal Allies," https://www.npr.org/2011/08/14/139619834.

were used as shields, early warnings for bombs, and gas detectors. In ancient Egypt, cats were worshipped, and killing one could cost you your life. Their high regard for the feline resulted in mummifying their remains. More than 300,000 mummified cats have been found. The Persians knew Egyptian soldiers could not kill cats and used this against them in the Battle of Pelusium in 525 BC. The Persians painted the image of Bastet, the Egyptian cat goddess, upon their shields and released cats upon the battlefield. Since Egyptians could not harm them, they surrendered.

During World War I, the British army used approximately 500,000 cats as gas detectors. The Germans first used poisonous gas to break the stalemate in trench warfare. It posed a disastrous threat to soldiers in World War I. Cats' smaller bodies reacted earlier to gas than humans, warning the latter of the danger. During World War II, cats served as early detectors for bomb attacks. They had an uncanny sense of detecting when a bomb was about to strike. People soon learned to follow their cats to bomb shelters. During 2022–2023, stray cats and dogs, along with those rescued from bombed villages in Ukraine, joined Ukrainian soldiers in the trenches, providing them with soothing companions that boosted morale. In the 1960s, the CIA spent 20 million dollars on "Project Acoustic Kitty" in a failed attempt to enable cats to be used to spy on the Soviets, especially their embassies. A microphone was implanted in the cat's ear, and a radio was at the skull's base. This would allow the cat to record and transmit sounds that occurred around it. The project was abandoned because of the cat's inability to stay focused because of hunger and its independent nature. This was not the only CIA project that failed. Other failures included dragonfly drones, robotic fish, and pigeons with mounted cameras. Despite these setbacks, the CIA contends it has not found an animal it could not train.[18]

During World War II in 1941, one cat named Sam survived three sinking ships. The first was sunk by a German ship. Five months later, Sam was on a British vessel that sunk, followed three weeks later by another torpedoed British boat. Sam was angry but unharmed. He had well-earned the name "Unsinkable Sam."[19]

Since the 1960s, the United States has made impressive strides in using dolphins and seals for military purposes. The United States Naval Marine Mammal Program uses bottlenose dolphins and California seals to track ships, detect mines, recover equipment, and amazingly, to capture enemy divers. When an enemy diver is found, the dolphin will approach him from behind, bumping into the air tank and attaching a line connected to a buoy, which then explodes. This alerts naval personnel, who retrieve the enemy diver. Sea lions have carried a line in their mouth, attaching it to the diver by handcuffing one of his limbs. Research by the Defense Advanced Research Projects Agency (DARPA) is working to make fish, shellfish, and other marine organisms into unwilling spies to find and track enemy submarines and other underwater threats.[20]

The British used exploding rats against the Germans in World War II. Dead rats filled with explosives were left near factories with

---

[18] "Acoustic Kitty," Wikipedia, https://en.wikipedia.org/wiki/Acoustic-kitty. Melissa Mills, "Heroic Cats Who Served in the Military," Reader's Digest, http://www.rd.com/list.military-cats. Sam Benson Smith, "The CIA Tried to Turn Cats into Secret Agents – and it Ended Badly," https://www.rd.com/aarticle/cats-as-secret-agents-cia. "How Caats Were Used in Warfare: FelinSoldiers,"https://worldhistory.us/military-history/how-cats. A British cat named Bomber could distinguish between the sounds made by British and German aircraft. The war in Ukraine has not only dislocated people but cats. Felines are overflowing facilities for their care.
[19] Jackie Mead, "6 Heroic Military Cats," www.mentalfloss.com/article/638468/cat-war-heroes. Unsinkable Sam retired from services and was put in a home in Gibraltar.
[20] Joseph Truvithick, "DARPA Wants to Use Fish and Other Sea Life to Track Enemy Submarines," https://www.reddit.com.>news>comment>dalpa_w; "United States Navy Marine Mammal Project," Wikipedia, https://en.wilipedia.org/wiki/United_States_Naval_Mammal_Program.

the hope the Germans would get rid of the carcasses by burning them in the factory's furnace, causing them to explode and inflict extensive damage. Rats' most significant role in war is the threat to the health of soldiers on both sides. The worst rat infestation was in the trenches on the Western Front in World War I. The massive amount of debris and filth led to an overwhelming number of rodents that many claimed were the size of cats. They were where the soldiers fought, slept, and ate, posing severe health hazards, such as spreading diseases and unending annoyance. Nocturnal rats were the most active at night when soldiers tried to sleep. Attempts to use poison threatened the health of soldiers, and although cats were ineffective in reducing their numbers, terrier dogs were effective. Once the war was over, the number of rats drastically declined. The difficulties rats posed in World War I's trenches led to avoiding using trenches in future wars. However, this did not prevent rodents from appearing on future battlegrounds. During the Korean War, rats were rampant in the bunkers of soldiers. Brian Hough, a British Army soldier with permanent scars from rat bites, remembers one night he saw his bunkmate "fast asleep with a rat on his chest gnawing at his clothing."[21]

    Swine are also an unlikely war animal. Their use as war animals was primarily during ancient warfare as a secret weapon against elephants. It was believed that elephants were afraid of squealing pigs. The Romans were reported to have used wild boars against the Tarantines in 272 BC and again to repel the war elephants of

---

21 "Military Animals," Wikipedia, https://en.wikipedia.org/wiki/military-animals. "Trench Rats," Wikipedia, https://en.wikipedia.org/wiki/Trench_rats; Zachary Matusheski, "Rats, Viruses and the Korean War," https://www.wearethemighty/history/r. Trainers contend that adaptability, intelligence, and focus make them one of the most accessible animals to train. They are being trained to carry a string attached to a computer cable for internet through holes in walls. Domestic rats are currently therapy animals for young people with developmental disabilities. In Belgium, an organization trains Gambian pouched rats, known as HeroRATs, to sniff out tuberculosis and land mines. HeroRATs are supported by hundreds of thousands of people who "adopt" them by committing to pay for their support.

the Greek king Pyrrhus. The defenders of Edessa, an ancient city in Mesopotamia, suspended a squealing pig on the city wall to scare away the elephants of their attackers.[22]

Most people would think chickens are one of the least likely war animals; indeed, experiments with them for combat use did not work out. Encouraged by using canaries' ability to detect poisonous gas in mines, the US military used chickens in the Gulf Wars to detect toxic gas. Like the canary, chickens and birds generally have delicate lungs, so their reaction time to poisonous gas is much shorter than humans. The use of chickens in both Gulf Wars was called "Operation Kuwaiti Field Chicken." During the first Gulf War, chickens were once placed outside a camp to detect poisonous gas. The following morning, they were all dead—not from the fumes of toxic gas but from the freezing temperatures. They tried using 43 chickens in the second Gulf War. The plan was to protect soldiers from poisonous gas by placing the chickens in cages on top of military vehicles. If the fowl suddenly died, the soldiers would return home. But before this could be done, 41 chickens suddenly died of unknown causes. They were buried with wooden tombstones marking their graves.[23]

During the Spanish Civil War in the 1930s, Nationalist pilots dropped turkeys with fragile supplies to their supporters. The turkeys' flapping wings during the fall served as a parachute. They also became a source of food.[24]

A lion and a baboon also rank as unusual war animals. Egyptian Ramesses II led Egyptian forces against the Hittites in one of the world's most significant chariot battles, the 1274 BC Battle

---

22   "War Pigs," Wikipedia, https://en.wikipedia.org/wiki/War_Pigs.
23   Jenny McCormick, "Chickens of the Gulf War –Operation Kuwaiti Field Chicken," https://www.premier1supplies.com/equipment.
24   "Military Animals," Wikipedia, https:en.wikipedia.org/wiki/Military_Animals.

of Kadesh in Syria. Ramesses' pet lion fought with him. Corporal Jackie, a baboon, fought in World War I. When his owner joined the South African Army, he took Jackie. The baboon became a mascot and fit right in. He was given a uniform and learned to salute superiors and light soldiers' cigarettes. The army gave Jackie rations, and he ate with the men using his knife and fork. He accompanied the men on marches and drills. When his owner was hurt in combat, Jackie licked his wound until help arrived. Later, Jackie was wounded in the shoulder and lost a leg. He was given the Medal of Honor and promoted to corporal. Although other baboons were in the South African Army, none reached his achievements.[25]

ANIMALS SENT ON SUICIDE MISSIONS

In warfare, animals have been used to save ally human lives, inflict oppositional damage, and take the lives of the enemy. War and the killing of humans blunted the standard sensitivities that might be prevalent during peacetime. Nevertheless, some animal use was brutally cruel, especially during ancient wars. Many schemes sacrificing animal life in combat failed.

One example of brutality is the use of incendiary pigs in 266 BC. When the king of Greece, Antigonus II Gonatas, laid siege to Megara, an ancient city in Greece, the defenders put combustibles like pitch, crude oil, and resin on pigs. They set them on fire, driving them toward the enemies' elephants. The giant beasts panicked when seeing and hearing the flaming and squealing hogs in intense pain, trampling and killing many of their soldiers.[26]

Unfortunate monkeys were also used as incendiary devices in China during the early Southern Song dynasty (960–1279). In a

---
25 "Corporal Jackie," Wikipedia, en.wikipedia.org/wiki/corporal_Jackie. "Military Animal."
26 "War pigs," Wikipedia, https:en.wikipedia.org/wiki/War-pigs.

battle between rebels and the Chinese Imperial Army, monkeys were clothed in straw, soaked in oil, and taken to the enemy camp. There, they were set on fire and loose in the enemy camp, burning tents and creating chaos.[27]

A similar and no less inhumane use of animals occurred during the Warring States era of Chinese history (fifth–third century BC). The Qi general, Tian Dan, dressed and painted 1,000 oxen as dragons, set their tails on fire, and herded them into the opposing Yan Army.

In the Second Punic War, during which Rome and Carthage fought, Hannibal, the Carthaginian general, attached torches to bulls' horns, set their tails on fire at night, and turned the flaming livestock loose. Thinking it was a Carthaginian retreat, Roman soldiers followed the light and were caught in an ambush.

Bombs attached to animals have been used by modern terrorists and insurgents in the Middle East. Sometimes, the animals wandered alone, and at other times, they were ridden by suicide bombers. During World War II, the US had Project Pigeon, which considered using pigeons to guide bombs.[28]

One of the wildest schemes was the British nuclear weapons project of the 1950s. The plan was to place nuclear land mines in Germany to blunt any Soviet invasion from the east. The Blue Peacock project ran into difficulty because frozen ground during the winter made the explosive device inoperable. One proposed solution was to place chickens with food and water with explosives to keep the device warm enough to be operable. The fowls were expected to live about a week. The nuclear land mines were to be detonated by a wire

---

27 "Military Animal," Wikipedia,https:en.wikipedia.org/wiki/military_animals.
28 Ibid.

three miles away, or an anti-tampering device. When the abandoned project became public, it was considered an "April Fools'" joke.[29]

The proposed use of cat bombs during World War II by the US Office of Strategic Services (forerunner of the CIA) ranks at least a close second to the Blue Peacock project in its bizarreness. It was based on the theory that cats could be used to improve the efficiency of the Air Force in targeting enemy warships. A cat was attached to a bomb and dropped in the ocean near an enemy vessel. Since cats hate to get wet, the theory was they would seek refuge by swimming to the enemy ship, enabling it to be sunk. The problematic issue of how a cat could swim pulling a bomb weighing hundreds of pounds became a moot issue. The project never got out of the experimental stage because once the cats were dropped from the plane, they passed out and sank into the ocean.[30]

Arguably more lucid, but certainly not more humane, was the Soviets' usage of anti-tank dogs in World War II. German Shepherds and other breeds were taught to carry explosives strapped to their backs and run under enemy tanks and other targets, incapacitating the vehicle and terminating the dog's life. The use of anti-tank dogs had limited success. Approximately 40,000 dogs were used by the Soviets during the war for various tasks. The use of anti-attack dogs led to several problems. They were trained to run under German tanks that sat still and had no gunfire. On the battlefield, dogs refused to run under moving tanks. Some ran to tanks but were shot while waiting for the tanks to stop. Others ran away, frightened by the tank's gunfire, and hurried back and jumped into the trenches, detonating the charge and killing Soviet soldiers. Handlers were forced to shoot their returning canines. Another negative was the dogs ran

---

[29] "Blue Peacock," Wikipedia.org/wiki/BluePeacock.
[30] Theunis Bates, "The Pentagon's 5 Most Ridiculous Projects," (theweek.com/articles/459802/pentagons-5-most ridiculous-projects).

toward what they were used to: Soviet tanks that used diesel fuel. The smell of gas-powered enemy tanks repelled them.[31]

The United States had an even less successful project during World War II, spending two million dollars on 6,000 bats in an attempt to create bat bombs. The plan was to arm and drop 1,000 live bats with incendiary devices in containers at dawn over a 20-40-mile area of Japan. Midway in the drop, the bats would be released from the containers, and a parachute would open. Upon landing, the bats would hopefully attach themselves to the eves and attics of wooden structures. Timers would set off incendiary devices to set the buildings on fire. Tests revealed that the bats dropped from airplanes just fell to the ground, and only a few structures burned, dooming the plan of using bat bombs.[32]

---

[31] "Anti-Tank Dog." Wikipedia, https://en.wikipedia.org/wiki/Anti-tank_dog.
[32] "Bat Bomb," Wikipedia, https://en.wikipedia.org/Bat_Bomb.

CHAPTER 2

RECRUITING THE CIVIL WAR'S MOST SIGNIFICANT ANIMALS

The American Civil War did not use all the unique war animals in the history of animals employed during wars. Still, it continued to use the horse as the predominant war animal, significantly supplemented by the mule. Author and student of the Civil War C. Kay Larson addresses the significance of the horse in the war in *The New York Times*, stating: "The Civil War is not normally called a horse's war, but it most certainly was . . ."[33]

Resources play a vital role in determining the outcome of wars. For the Civil War, these included population, equipment, and animals. The Union had far more advantages than the Confederacy. The North had four times the men of military age, an established government, the country's banking center, a better-balanced economy, 92 percent of the industry, double the railroad mileage, and more draft animals, except mules, than the South. There were 4,600,000 horses, mules, and asses in the North compared to 2,566,000 draft animals in the South. The South had almost three times the number of mules.

---

[33] Michael Mountain, "Horses in the Civil War," https:www.earthintransition.org/.

The war would drag on for four bloody years. Confederate leaders knew this resource disparity and sought Europe's help, believing the South held the trump card: "King Cotton." England, the world's largest producer of textiles, whose dependence upon Southern cotton could not be obtained elsewhere, led Southerners to believe England would be forced to aid the Confederacy by recognizing the South's independence, mediating an end of the war or intervening militarily. None of these happened, dooming King Cotton's diplomacy. One of the factors leading to its failure was England's cotton surplus at the start of the war and obtaining cotton from Egypt and India.[34]

EQUINE WARRIORS

No animal has played a more significant role in man's mobility than the horse. For centuries, horses have been a crucial component in humans' lives during peacetime and war. Horses likewise played an essential role in the Civil War. The technological advancements of the Industrial Revolution would make horses' traditional role in combat and on the farm obsolete, but initially, it accelerated the need for and use of the equine.

Railroads, an integral part of the industrial revolution, were crucial in increasing the need for horses. The horse was needed to move the products of industrialization the rail lines carried. War further increased the demand for them. Many horses accompanied Union and Confederate forces, providing mounts for cavalry units and officers, power for pulling white-covered supply wagons and artillery, and protection for vulnerable rail lines from the enemy and telegraph lines paralleling the tracks. The size of the armies, too large to live off the land and away from rail lines, necessitated an army's support be carried with them. Among the many support

---

34 Donald B. Cole, *Handbook of American History* (New York: Harcourt, Brace & World, 1968), 128.

items needed was bulky and heavy animal feed. The daily rations for a horse, which they frequently did not get, were 14 pounds of hay (unbaled) and 12 pounds of grain. To transport these swelled the number of horses, mules, and wagons needed for the movement of many soldiers. Four horses, or six mules, pulled a 12-foot-long wagon, needing 50 feet of road space. Some wagon trains were eight miles long. Union quartermaster trains had an average of one wagon for every 24 soldiers. Providing food and equipment for the artillery and cavalry required one horse or mule for every two men. Hay and grain for animals comprised more than half of what wagon trains carried.

The Union Army used more mules as draft animals as the war progressed because they were more durable than horses. During the war, the Union purchased approximately one million mules. Their principal task was pulling wagons. During the Gettysburg campaign, the Union had 4,300 wagons, 21,000 mules, 8,889 draft horses, and 216 pack mules. The size of mules and their skittishness under fire made them rarely used for pulling field guns, but the sturdy and durable mule was a valuable pack animal.

Field artillery also needed horses. For example, an eight-gun battery required six horses to pull each artillery piece. In addition to the 96 horses needed to move a battery's artillery, five teams of horses or mules were required to pull support wagons (forge wagons, battery wagons, and three supply wagons). They also had additional horses for cannoneers to ride.[35]

---

35   Thomas A. Bailey, *A Diplomatic History of The American People* (New York: Appleton-Century-Crofts, 1955), 360-362. T. Harry Williams, Richard N. Current and Frank Freidel, *A History of the United States* (New York: Alfred A. Knopf, 1960), vol 1, 392-393.

ACQUIRING FOUR-LEGGED WARRIORS

War rapidly diminished resources that included both humans and animals. Most Civil War soldiers were volunteers stimulated by bounties and supplemented in the middle of the war with the hated draft when volunteering lagged. The most valuable living resource in the Civil War, next to humans, was horses. Both were increasingly needed, especially in the Confederacy, as casualties mounted as the war dragged on. Getting the required quality and quantity was an ongoing issue throughout the war. For the Union, it was more a problem of quality than quantity, and for the Confederacy, it was a problem of both. An example of the extensive need for replacement horses for the Union Army in 1864 was the need for 500 new horses daily.

There were four primary methods of obtaining horses and mules for the military: purchasing them, capturing them from the enemy, seizing them (impressment) from civilians, and bringing your own. The Union armies used approximately 825,766 purchased horses. They bought them by contracts with dealers that stated the price per head, which averaged $140. Confederates also purchased equines, but cavalrymen, unlike the Union, brought their own horses. This changed in 1863, and the Confederate government purchased mounts for troopers. Both combatants captured them from each other and took them from civilians, frequently not paying for them.

Quartermaster General Montgomery Meigs was responsible for acquiring many horses needed for the Union and additional tasks, such as ordnance, soldiers' rations, and medical needs. It was a formidable task, which he did, but at the cost of almost two billion dollars, of which $124,000,000 was for horses and mules. No centralized market existed for the horses and mules scattered throughout the North. The lack of a central market resulted in vast numbers of people in the US military and state governors having the authority to purchase horses for the Union by sealed bids. However, unlike the Confederates, the Union had a centralized procurement organization with the quartermaster department supplying horses. To do this, the Cavalry Bureau was created in July 1863. The contract system obtained around 650,000 horses during the war for the Union, and an additional 75,000 were seized in Confederate territory.

At the beginning of the war, the value of horses in the Union and Confederacy was about the same, averaging between $100 and $145, with artillery horses later selling for $185. Demand increased prices as the war continued, roughly doubling the replacement cost for the Union and accelerating the expense for Confederates to $500 to $600 a horse, a fivefold increase.

All horses and mules were inspected before the sale was final. It was subjective and included looking at their teeth to estimate their age. Greedy and dishonest dealers and appraisers distorted the process far from any hint of reality. They worked together to drive up prices and failed to provide healthy gelding at the desired age of four to nine years or mules over 14 hands and two years of age. Worse, they sent horses with bad hooves, blindness, and other disqualifying conditions. Some horses looked fine but became incapacitated after a brief military service. Meigs was forced when additional horses and mules were critically needed to knowingly purchase inferior animals that would last only a week or two. Corruption in the procurement process was costly and not only existed in procuring horses but throughout the procurement system in the North early in the war. Fred A. Shannon pointed out: "Through haste, carelessness, or criminal collusion, the state and federal officers accepted almost every offer and paid almost any price for commodities, regardless of character, quantity, or quantity." This was elaborated further by *Harper's Magazine*: "For sugar it [the government] often got sand; for coffee, rye; for leather, something no better than brown paper; for sound horse and mules, spavined beasts, and dying donkeys; and serviceable muskets and pistols, the experimental failures of sanguine inventors, or the refuse of shops and foreign armories."[36]

As the war continued, impressment increased for both combatants, which occurred primarily in the theaters of the war. Southern forces were forced to start impressment first as the Union increasingly gained control of parts of the Confederacy, like middle Tennessee, which reduced their territory for obtaining equines. Disgruntled farmers and merchants were forced to give up animals and produce in exchange for IOU receipts or the limited value of paper money. Farmers hid their crops and drove livestock into the woods to prevent seizures. To some Southern farmers, the sight of Confederate cavalry was more disheartening than the appearance of the enemy. When the war ended, Southerners were stuck with approximately half a billion dollars of unpaid receipts.[37]

---

36   Gene C. Armistead, *Horses and Mules in the Civil War* (Jefferson, NC: McFarland & Company, 2013), 20. Judson Browning and Timothy Silver, *An Environmental History of the Civil War* (Chapel Hill: University of North Carolina Press, 2020), 107. Ann Norton Greene, *Horses at Work* (Cambridge, Massachusetts, 2008), 121-125, 135-141. Emmett M. Essin, *Shavetails & Bell Sharps* (Lincoln, Nebraska: University of Nebraska Press, 1997), 69, 73, 81. J. B. Polley, *A Soldier's Letters To Charming Nellie* (New York: Neale Publishing Company, 1908), 95-96. Fred A. Shannon, *The Organization and Administration of the Union Army 1861-1865*, (Gloucester, MA: 1965), vol. 1, 55-56. *The War Of Rebellion: A Compilation of the Official Records of the Union and Confederate Armies* (Washington, D. C.: Government Printing Office, 1881). Ser. III, Vol. 5, 1212. (Hereafter referred to as *OR*). Greene, *Horses at Work*, 127-134. Nancy F. McEntee, *Haversacks, Hardtack, And Unserviceable Mules* (Maryville, Tennessee, 2017), 168. Meigs had to obtain mundane items like pins and buttons to steamboats, railroad cars, ambulances, pontoon bridges, and clothing. The prices for horses varied. Inspectors examined a horse or mule's teeth to determine their age. In horses, they looked for the wear of the teeth, and for mules, if they lost their front teeth, it meant it was over two years old.
37   *Journal of the Congress of the Confederate States of America, 1861-1865* (Washington: Government Printing Office, 1904), 37-38, vol. III. James M. McPherson, *Ordeal By Fire* (New York: Alfred A. Knopf, 1982) 378. To regulate impressment, the Confederate government enacted the Impressment Act of 1863.

Confederates had a form they issued to those whose property they seized. An example is the following given during 1863 to obtain beeves and bacon from a farmer in Florida:

> OFFICE DISTRICT COMMISSARY, SECOND DISTRICT,
> Tallahassee, Fla., November, 1863.
>
> Mr. G. D. CHAIRES:
>
> SIR: The head of beeves and pounds of bacon which you now have on hand is needed for the use of the armies of the Confederate States. For this purpose I will pay you at the rate of schedule price per ——.
>
> If this price is not satisfactory to you compensation for the property will be made according to the act of Congress passed for the regulation of impressments; and you are hereby notified that in pursuance of the provisions of said act the Government requires you to hold said property subject to my order, and not to remove it until the business be concluded between us in terms of the law in such case made and provided.
>
> This notice is intended to be applied to all bacon and beeves, and any other article of subsistence required for the use of the Army in your possession, giving marks, description of packages, and by whom owned, as in the event of your failure so to do it will become my duty to make the forcible search and seizure authorized by law.
>
> By order of Maj. A. B. Noyes, district commissary:
> Very respectfully, your obedient servant,
>
> M. S. ELKIN,
> Commissary Agent.

Many others also received this form, which caused Governor John Milton to send a lengthy written protest to the Confederate Congress in 1863 to protect citizens from this governmental abuse.

Ninety-two articles could be appropriated from Southerners by impressment. The extensive and abusive use of impressment of horses caused Confederate authorities to issue an order stating the "appropriation by the impressment of horses . . . without warrant of law . . . will not be allowed."[38]

The following prices were the maximum rates the Southern government would pay in 1864.

---

38 *OR*, Ser. IV, vol. 2, 972-976. *OR*, Ser. III, vol. 3, 369.

	Article.	Quality.	Description.	Quantity.	Price.
1	Wheat	Prime	White or red	Per bushel of 60 pounds	$5.00
2	Flour	Good	Fine	Per barrel of 196 pounds	22.00
	do	do	Superfine	do	25.00
	do	do	Extra superfine	do	26.50
	do	do	Family	do	28.00
3	Corn	Prime	White or yellow	Per bushel of 56 pounds	4.00
4	Corn, unshelled	do	do		3.95
5	Corn-meal	Good		Per bushel of 50 pounds	4.20
6	Rye	Prime		Per bushel of 56 pounds	3.20
7	Cleaned oats	do		Per bushel of 32 pounds	2.50
8	Wheat bran	Good		Per bushel of 17 pounds	.50
9	Shorts	do		Per bushel of 22 pounds	.70
10	Brown stuff	do		Per bushel of 28 pounds	.90
11	Ship stuff	do		Per bushel of 37 pounds	1.40
12	Bacon	Good	Hog round	Per pound	$1.25
13	Pork, salt	do		do	1.10
	Pork, fresh	Fat and good		Per pound, net weight	.80
14	Lard	Good		Per pound	1.25
15	Horses	First class	Artillery, &c	Average price per head	350.00
16	Wool	Fair or merino	Washed	Per pound	3.00
17	do	do	Unwashed	do	2.00
18	Peas	Good		Per bushel	4.00
19	Beans	do		do	4.00
20	Potatoes	do	Irish	do	4.00
21	do	do	Sweet	do	5.00
22	Onions	do		do	5.00
23	Peaches, dried	do	Peeled	do	8.00
24	do	do	Unpeeled	do	4.50
25	Apples, dried	do	Peeled	do	3.00
26	Hay, baled	do	Timothy or clover	Per 100 pounds	3.50
27	do	do	Orchard or herd grass	do	3.00
28	Hay, unbaled	do	do	do	3.00
29	Sheaf oats, baled	do		do	4.00
30	Sheaf oats, unbaled	do		do	3.50
31	Blade fodder, baled	do		do	3.50
32	Blade fodder, unbaled	do		do	3.00
33	Shucks, baled	do		do	2.20
34	Shucks, unbaled	do		do	1.70
35	Wheat straw, baled	do		do	1.80
36	Wheat straw, unbaled	do		do	1.30
37	Pasturage	do	Interior	Per head per month	3.00
38	do	Superior	do	do	4.00
39	do	First rate	do	do	5.00
40	do	Good	Near cities	do	5.00
41	do	Superior	do	do	6.00
42	do	First rate	do	do	7.00
43	Salt	Good		Per bushel of 50 pounds	5.00
44	Soap	do		Per pound	.40
45	Candles	do	Tallow		2.00
46	Vinegar	do	Cider	Per gallon	2.00
47	Whisky	do	Trade	do	3.00
48	Sugar	do	Brown	Per pound	1.50
49	Molasses	do	New Orleans	Per gallon	10.00
50	Rice	do		Per pound	.20
51	Coffee	do	Rio	do	3.00
52	Tea	do	Trade	do	7.00
53	Vinegar	do	Manufactured	Per gallon	.50
54	Pig-iron	do	No. 1 quality	Per ton	150.00
55	do	do	No. 2 quality	do	132.00
56	do	do	No. 3 quality	do	120.00
57	Bloom iron	do		do	216.00
58	Smith's iron	do	Round, plate, and bar	do	456.00
59	Railroad iron	do		do	190.00
60	Leather	do	Harness	Per pound	2.60
61	do	do	Sole	do	2.40
62	do	do	Upper	do	2.80
63	Beef-cattle	do	Gross weight	Per 100 pounds	16.00
64	do	Superior	do	do	18.00
65	do	First rate	do	do	20.00
66	Sheep	Fair		Per head	30.00
67	Army woolen cloth, 3-4 yard	Good	10 ounces per yard	Per yard	5.00
68	Army woolen cloth	do			(a)
69	Army woolen cloth, 6-4 yard	do	20 ounces per yard	Per yard	10.00
70	Army woolen cloth	do			(a)
71	Flannels, 3-4	do	6 ounces per yard	Per yard	4.00
72	Cotton shirting, 3-4	do	4½ yards to pound	do	.56
73	Cotton shirting, 7-8	do	3¾ yards to pound	do	.84
74	Cotton sheetings, 4-4	do	3 yards to pound	do	.87
75	Cotton, Osnaburg, 3-4	do	6 ounces per yard	do	.75
76	Cotton, Osnaburg, 7-8	do	8 ounces per yard	do	.88
77	Cotton drills, 7-8	do	3 yards to pound	do	.88
78	Cotton shirting stripes	do		do	.88
79	Cotton tent cloths	do	10 ounces per yard	do	1.12
80					(b)
81	Cotton warps	Good		Per pound	2.00
82	Army shoes	do		Per pair	10.00
83	Shoe thread	do		Per pound	2.00
84	Wool socks, men's	do		Per pair	1.25
85	Mules	First rate	Wagon, &c	Average price per head	300.00
86	Corntop fodder, baled	Good		Per 100 pounds	2.00
87	Corntop fodder, unbaled	do		do	1.50
88	Wheat chaff, baled	Good		Per 100 pounds	$2.00
89	Wheat chaff, unbaled	do		do	1.50
90	Sorghum molasses	do		Per gallon	8.00
91	Pasturage for sheep	do	Interior	Per head	.40
92	do	Superior	do	do	.50
93	do	First rate	do	do	.60

The Southern problem of obtaining livestock and supplies was more than shortages. It also involved the South's inability to finance the war, a critical factor in losing it. Charles W. Ramsdell stated, "The Confederacy had begun to crumble, or break down within, long before the military situation appeared desperate." The Union and Confederacy financed the war through loans, taxes, and paper money. Specie (metal money) disappeared in both the North and South. The Union depended on loans supplemented by taxes and paper money, whereas the South tried to finance the war with paper money supplemented by taxes and loans. The excessive printing of paper money by the Confederate and state governments, cities, banks, and counterfeiters depreciated the value of their paper money as almost worthless. Even beggars in Richmond, Virginia, would not accept paper money less than $5.00. By the war's end, the South suffered from a 9,000 percent increase in inflation compared to an 80 percent increase in the North, similar to that of both world wars.[39]

The increasing worthlessness of paper money and the need for sustenance for the men and animals of the military forced the Confederacy in 1863 to use a tax in kind that had to be paid in farm products collected by arbitrary government agents. After deducting the number of food crops needed for their family, farmers had to pay the government one-tenth of their remaining crops and bacon. The crops paid in taxes included cotton, sugar, corn, wheat, tobacco, peas, and forage (hay and fodder). Southerners hated all taxes, including the tax in kind. Farm products were not uniformly collected throughout the South, and those that were collected frequently perished at railroad stations waiting to be picked up. Tax in kind at best provided temporary help. To compensate for the lack of revenue from taxes, the Confederate government instituted the loan

---

39   Clement Eaton, *A History of the Southern Confederacy* (New York: Free Press, 1954), 227. *Journal of the Confederate States of America*, 67, 125, vol. II. McPherson, *Ordeal By Fire*, 199-205.

in kind, also known as produce loans, where farm products were sent to the Confederate government in exchange for bonds.[40] Like the tax in kind, loans in kind did little to solve the South's economic crisis.

The weakness of the economy, especially inflation, shackled the Confederate government, civilians, and those in the military. Like their Union counterparts, those who owned their horses were compensated 40 cents a day. A cavalryman who lost his mount because it had been disabled or killed became a Company Q member. He was a cavalryman without a horse forced to remain in the dismounted camp, described by a Confederate officer as where "hundreds of men were collected in a useless crowd."[41] A Confederate member of Company Q had to return home for another mount, which took time away from military service, or purchase a new horse. Inflation accelerated the cost far above what the cavalrymen or officers received from the government for losing their mount or the horse's value at the start of its service. Confederates capped the maximum payment at $200 as scarcity, and rising costs were three to four times the compensation amount. Many cavalrymen were repeatedly dismounted, losing up to five horses. The situation became desperate to the point President Jefferson Davis asked Quartermaster General A. C. Myers about purchasing horses and mules from Mexico, California, and Europe. Myers responded, "If they are judiciously selected," and "none are purchased under ten years of age. Unbroken Mexican horses, I consider entirely useless. The proposal to obtain horses from Europe is impracticable." Others claimed the only solution for additional horses was to take horses from the enemy. The lack of

---

40 Francis Trevelyan Miller, ed., *The Photographic History of the Civil War: The Cavalry* (New York: The Review of Reviews Co., 1911), vol 10, p. 38.
41 J. William Jones, ed., *Southern Historical Society Papers* (Richmond, VA: Southern Historical Society, 1884, 170 (Hereafter referred to as *SHSP*). OR Ser. IV, vol 2, 416-417.

horses led to using animals of limited use, like donkeys, and confiscating children's ponies.[42]

Although not as severe as the Confederate need for mounts, it became a recurring and critical problem for the Union. Just one of many examples is indicated in the situation of a Union colonel who had lost more than half of his horses in several engagements. When he appealed to the quartermaster for remounts, he received the reply, "Colonel, I'll tell you frankly that we haven't five pounds of horse for each man." Testily, the colonel responded, "That won't help much; we were thinking of riding the brutes, not eating them."

Desperation for more horses led to unrestrained impressment not only by the Confederates but also by the Union. In 1864, General James H. Wilson desperately needed horses for his cavalry to keep Confederates under General John B. Hood's forces in check near Nashville while Sherman marched to the sea. Union Secretary of War Edwin Stanton gave orders to impress horses from people south of the Ohio River, giving them vouchers for each horse taken. In seven days, the Union swept up 12,000 horses. Every horse that could be used was taken; livery, streetcar, carriage, saddle, and circus horses were seized. Even Vice President-elect Andrew Johnson had two horses impressed.[43]

Like horses, mules became more challenging to obtain. The states that had the most mules were Kentucky, Missouri, and Tennessee. They had what was considered the best in quality and size. The shrinking Confederacy led to a diminishing source of these long-eared creatures and forced the Southern military to

---

42 Miller, *The Photographic History of the Civil War*, 326.
43 Sue Cottrell, *Hoof Beats North and South* (Hicksville, New York: Exposition Press, 1975), 15-16. OR, Ser. IV, vol 2, 416-417. Jonathan R. Allen, "Civil War Mules," http://www.nellaware.com>blog>civil-war-mules. E. B. Long, *The Civil War Day by Day* (Garden City, New York: Doubleday & Company), 601-604.

look elsewhere, including Mexico and Europe. In March 1863, Confederate Quartermaster Myers told President Davis they had purchased 600 to 700 mules from Texas, but that only time would reveal how useful they were since they were small. The consequences of the lack of mules got worse. One example is the extensive Confederate losses to the enemy as they retreated after their brutal defeat in late 1864 in the Battle of Franklin, Tennessee. During the retreat, the Confederates lost 72 pieces of artillery and hundreds of wagons because they lacked mules to pull them.

The difficulty of getting a horse also plagued civilians from the start of the war. This included news correspondents. Before the First Battle of Bull Run, a Washington liveryman charged the *London Times* correspondent William H. Russell $1,000 for a spavined horse with a diseased (swollen) hock joint in a back leg between the knee and fetlock. The liveryman told Russell to "take it or leave it. If you want to see this fight, a thousand dollars is Cheap." If you had a horse, the thief made it hard to keep. The correspondent for *The Boston Journal*, Charles Carleton Coffin, had a striking mount frequently stolen. He was often awakened in the morning by a negro employee who stuck his head in the tent with the greeting, "Breakfast is ready, Mr. Coffin, your horse is gone again."[44]

CARE AND TREATMENT

The inability to get mounts was a significant factor in the Confederate cavalry's losing its domination over the Union it held the first half of the war. The Federals' delay in realizing the value of cavalry also aided the Southerners' early superiority. At the beginning of the war, federal authorities limited the force of the Union cavalry to six regiments. General Winfield Scott's opinion was that

---

44   J. Cutler Andrews, *The North Reports The Civil War* (Pittsburgh: University of Pittsburgh Press, 1955), 64. Miller, *The Photographic History of the Civil War*, 50.

the cavalry would be unimportant and secondary due to the nature of the topography, which was broken and wooded.[45] This caused a delay in developing the organization to take care of the cavalry. Despite their early superiority, Confederates would not create an organization like the Federals later created.

The demand for horses would rapidly change the view of the insignificance of the cavalry. White horses were less desired because they stood out and showed dirt more than other colored equines. The early attempts by the Union to organize the cavalry according to the color of the horse—blacks, grays, bays, and sorrels—rapidly shifted to the priority of getting suitable mounts and, as the war continued, to accept anything identified as a horse. Due to the dwindling of his cavalry in the Peninsular Campaign, General McClellan wrote General Halleck in the fall of 1862: "It is necessary that some energetic measures be taken to supply the cavalry with remounts horses." The demand for horses frequently forced the Union to use exhausted animals without adequate time to recover from fatigue. Such was the case where exhausted horses were left in cars after a long railway trip of 50 hours. During that time, they were without food and water. When taken from the railroad cars, they were immediately sent into service.

The need for horses was expressed in the continual Union complaints about the quality of horses and the inadequacy in rehabilitating broken-down horses. Finally, the Union established the Cavalry Bureau in 1863. The bureau was charged with providing equipment for the cavalry, mounts and remounts, and the inspection of horses by experienced cavalry officers. The purchasing of horses remained under the quartermaster's department. Six depots were established for the reception, organization, and discipline of cavalry

---

45   Ibid., 322-330. Giesboro handled 170,622 horses in 1864. Its maximum capacity was 30,000. This included a hospital that could handle 2,650 animals.

recruits, horses' care, and training: Giesboro, Maryland; St. Louis, Missouri; Greenville, Louisiana; Nashville, Tennessee; Harrisburg, Pennsylvania; and Wilmington, Delaware. The largest depot was Giesboro, which comprised 625 acres of rented land on the bank of the Potomac River south of Washington, D.C.

On that site, wharves, forage houses, mess houses, storehouses, quarters, a grist mill, a chapel, and 32 large stables for 6,000 horses were constructed to care for up to 30,000 animals provided by 1,500 employees. The workers included blacksmiths, carpenters, wagon makers, carpenters, wheelwrights, farriers, teamsters, and laborers. The majority of the stock was in stockyards that covered 45 acres. Each had an open shed, hay racks, watering troughs, and access to the Potomac River. Giesboro had, on average, 5,000 to 10,000 horses requiring approximately 100 tons of hay and 60 tons of grain each day while also producing 200 tons of manure, much of which had to be removed by hand from stables.

The primary purpose of the six remount stations was to receive new horses and prepare them for military service. When the Cavalry Bureau was created, troopers needing remounts went to the dismounted camp near Giesboro to wait for a new horse and equipment. The dismount camp was a comfortable place where members, known as "coffee coolers," stayed waiting for new mounts. The camp was so appealing to cavalrymen that they intentionally lost their equipment and neglected their horses to return to the comfort of the dismounted camp. To prevent this, all horses and equipment were forwarded to the men in the field.

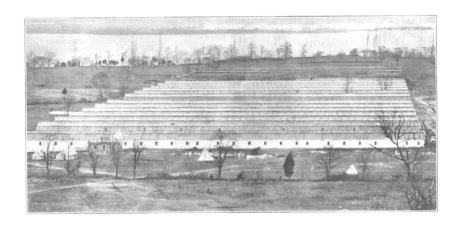

Shelter for horses at Giesboro cavalry depot south of Washington, D.C. The Potomac River is in the background. (Library of Congress)

Despite the primary purpose of the six depots, called "remount depots," much time was spent trying to mend sick and worn-down horses. Despite their size, horses are fragile creatures. They succumb to many diseases due to the lack of proper nutrition and care and the rigors of military service.

One of the many corrals at Giesboro, Maryland (Library of Congress)

The Union cavalry depots rehabilitated about half of the horses, classified as serviceable or convalescents. The rest were put in the unserviceable or condemned classification. Most of the condemned were sold at public auctions. One-fourth were severely ill and suffering animals. They either died at the depot or were killed to end their misery.[46]

---

46   Armistead, *Horses and Mules in the Civil* War, 63.

The Confederates exaggerated their success but had far less success rehabilitating equines than the Federals. Southern leadership recognized the need for rehabilitation centers and in 1863, established camps in four infirmary districts in the Confederacy. The Confederate horse infirmaries were similar to the remount camps of the Union. The largest was at Lynchburg, Virginia. Unfortunately, horses were frequently only sent to the infirmary in seriously debilitated shape, many suffering from a fatal disease. Less than 16 percent recovered and went back into service. Mules had a higher survival rate, partly because they were sent to camp earlier because it increased their chance of returning to service.[47]

Veterinary science was in its infancy, and lacking veterinarians diminished the rehabilitation success rates of camps on both sides. At the beginning of the war, both governments were indifferent to medical care for soldiers and animals. The brutality of war forced them to address this issue. Only 50 college-educated veterinarians were in the country when the war started. The Union spent only $168.50 on hiring civilian veterinarians for the first year of the war. Farriers and blacksmiths who cared for horses and had limited knowledge of treating horses were the closest thing they had to a veterinarian. The number of veterinarians increased for Union forces during the war's latter years, spurred by need and congressional legislation. On paper, each of the more than two hundred cavalry regiments was to have a veterinarian. There was a shortage of talent for veterinarians who were college-trained. This led to blacksmiths and farriers being selected by the government to fulfill the role of and being called veterinarians. Too often, the care of horses was left to the untrained. In 1862, the 3rd Pennsylvania Cavalry Regiment received many remounts; many were Sickly. Lacking a veterinarian, the commanding officer selected

---

[47] Armistead, *Horses and Mules*, 65. Nancy F. McEntee, *Haversacks, Hardtack, and Unserviceable Mules*, 169. Miller, *The Photographic History of the Civil War*, 42. OR, Ser. III, vol. 4, 198-199.

five volunteers to care for the horses, instructing them they would find the appropriate medicine and treatment in a book titled *Every Man His Own Horse Doctor*, published in 1738. None of the volunteers knew horses, so they mixed up a concoction that killed half of the remounts.[48]

Not only were horses vulnerable to diseases that debilitated thousands, but the lack of proper care, especially by inexperienced Union cavalrymen, led to sore backs, making mounts unrideable. Crude saddles rubbed backs raw. Cavalrymen soon learned to smooth out wrinkles in the saddle blanket carefully, rest jaded and exhausted animals, walk up steep hills, remove the saddle to cool the back of the horse after long rides, and carefully monitor how much water a horse had after a long march. The failures of inexperienced Union cavalrymen ignorant of proper horse care cost the Union government millions. Union Officer Charles D. Rhodes stated: "Comparatively few horses were destroyed by wounds on the battlefield as compared with the lost through the ignorance of troopers as to the proper method of resting a horse, and as to the science of how, when, and what to feed them, and when to allow him to drink and how much." General Meigs complained about the Union soldiers' lack of proper treatment of horses, stating: "We have over 126 regiments of cavalry, and they have killed ten times as many horses for us as for the Rebels." Improper care from ignorance and neglect was a significant problem for both sides, provoking Union authorities to take punitive action, transferring from the cavalry to the infantry, "any mounted man whose horse is, through his fault, and neglect, rendered unfit for service."[49]

---

48 Walter R. Heiss, *Veterinary Service During The American Civil War* (Baltimore, MD: Publish America, 2005), 16-17, 20-33.
49 Armistead, *Horses and Mules*, 60. One explanation for the hay wharf across the Potomac River from Giesboro was the danger of fire.

Water and food were essential for animals to perform their military duties. Horses and mules required ten gallons of water a day. So, military plans had to include its availability. What was fed to a horse, and the amount, was significant in maintaining equine health, but as the war lengthened, the shortage and poor quality of forage and grain for both sides became more critical. The lack of feed incapacitated equines and delayed both combatants from carrying out battle plans. By 1864, the Union had established a system for transporting hay to its forces. This included a large hay wharf at Alexandria, Virginia, where many laborers worked, sending hay to troops in the field.[50]

A Union hay wharf in Alexandria, Virginia. (Library of Congress)

The shortage of forage restricted the number of horses for officers the government would provide forage for. The higher-ranking Confederate officers could have several mounts. Confederates issued

---
50   Miller, *The Photographic History of the Civil War*, 65-67. OR, Ser. IV, vol. 2, 272.

forage to officers in the field for more than one horse, but those not on the front would receive forage for only one horse. In place of forage, eight dollars a month was given to each officer for each horse to which he was entitled. In 1862, the US Congress started rationing forage by limiting, according to rank, the number of horses the government would provide forage for: five for major generals, four for brigadier generals, two each for colonels and majors, and two for captains and lieutenants of cavalry and artillery.[51]

Next to the significance of getting proper food to the equines was caring for their feet. Federal Officer Charles Rhodes succinctly stated, "An army marches upon its stomach, but cavalry marches upon its horses' feet."[52] Mules and especially horses' hooves were sensitive and subject to painful and disabling infections and inflammations often caused by standing in mud, including hoof rot (thrush), grease heel (mud fever), and founder (laminitis), where the sole of the hoof separates from the wall.[53]

Horseshoes were essential to the health and mobility of horses and mules. Those unshod were called "shoeless" and soon became lame from extensive travel as their hooves pounded on hard surfaces while carrying rider and equipment that weighed 170 pounds. The shoeing frequency depended on the travel frequency, the road and field condition, the hooves' hardness or softness, and how fast they grew. Shoe sizes varied and were traditionally made by a blacksmith who labored for hours over a sweltering hot forge, preferably burning smokeless coke with a higher heat value than coal, reaching 2,000 degrees, vigorously pounding iron on an anvil into properly shaped horseshoes. Having a sufficient number of horseshoes and farriers to shod and reshod countless numbers of horses became an

---

51 *OR,* Ser. III, vol. 2, 277.
52 Miller, *The Photographic History of the Civil War,* 45.
53 Armistead, *Horses and Mules,* 62.

issue that plagued Southern forces. Horses frequently threw a shoe, and the scarcity of horseshoes made cavalrymen cut off the hooves of dead horses with horseshoes and carry them back to camp. The Union was fortunate not to have a shortage of horseshoes thanks to Henry Burden, who used a machine to mass-produce horseshoes at 3,600 an hour, providing the Union with an adequate supply throughout the war. Not having this source, Confederates hired spies in an unsuccessful attempt to replicate Burden's machine and struggled throughout the conflict to get the iron, nails, and coke needed to make horseshoes by hand.

Once the horseshoe is made, it requires skill to attach to the horse's hoof. Ineptness could lame a horse or mule. After the hoof is cleaned and filed to make it level and the proper size shoe is selected, it is nailed through the hole made in the shoe to the hoof. The hoof is comparable to a toenail in that they both grow, have to be trimmed, and have a keratin covering to protect the toe. Although the hoof is much thicker, it is still a narrow outside part of the foot, which the nail penetrates and is bent over and filed. A nail too far inward would damage the soft tissue of the foot. The shortage of horseshoes, blacksmiths, and farriers for the Confederacy and the Union's lack of this problem inspired clinical veterinary anatomist David Bainbridge to author an article titled "How Horseshoes Help Win the Civil War."[54]

---

54 David A. Bainbridge, "How Horseshoes Helped Win the Civil War." https://www.americanfarriers.com/article/12850.

A man shoeing a Union horse at Grant's headquarters at City Point in 1864. The grindstone was used to sharpen sabers. (Library of Congress)

A photograph picturing approximately half of the more than 100 men at Giesboro who shod a million horses. (Library of Congress)

How to shoe a mule (*Frank Leslie's Illustrated Newspaper*)

Caring for horses' backs was a close second to caring for their feet. A sore back made the horse unrideable. Significant causes of disablement were improper care by the rider and improperly fitting saddles. Saddles have a frame made of wood called a saddle tree. Early saddles were covered with rawhide, and later leather. Attached are a leather shirt, stirrups, and a girth strap of woolen yarn. Early in the war, Confederates brought their horses and saddles. Soon, their Ordnance Department provided the Jenifer saddle. When the Confederate mounts became thin with bony withers from inadequate food, the Jenifer saddle became painful and rubbed the horses' backs raw. Troopers damned the saddle. This led to Confederates shifting to their modification of the McClellan saddle, which was also denounced, a view that was forcefully articulated during the summer of 1863 in a report to a superior officer by Colonel John R. Chambliss, commanding Lee's cavalry brigade:

The saddles issued by the Ordnance Department are dreaded, ridiculed, and avoided by officers and men, and are used only through necessity, seldom without proving ruinous to the backs of horses. Though samples of the best approved saddles can be had anywhere, it is strange that no trees [saddles] can be manufactured comparable to the McClellan saddles, when as much time and material is consumed in constructing the miserable apologies issued to the cavalry in imitation of the above-named saddles. It would seem that a board of suitable and enterprising officers would take pleasure in instituting inquiry on the subject and in arresting the useless waste of material in the manufacture of these Confederate saddles.[55]

The Union cavalry had the superior McClellan saddle designed by a future commander of the Federal Army. Several years before the Civil War, Captain George B. McClellan spent a year in Europe, where he studied their methods of warfare and observed battles during the Crimean War. Back in the United States, he proposed a saddle that he claimed was a modification of a Hungarian model used by the Prussians. However, authorities contend it modified the Spanish saddle used in Mexico. Regardless of its heritage, the McClellan saddle has a long life and was used throughout both World Wars.[56]

---

55   OR, Ser. IV, vol. 2, 719.
56   "McClellan Saddle," Wikipedia, htttps://en.wiki.org>wiki>McClellan saddle. Armistead, *Horses and Mules in the Civil War,* 33.

CHAPTER 3

TRAINING, DEPLOYMENT, AND WEAPONRY

The behavior and knowledge needed in combat required training for both men and equines. It was a period of adjustment. Men had to learn new terms, take orders, perform drills, and accept a life controlled by others. This did not sit well for some, as they resented the officer they believed was below their social status. Although historically always controlled by humans, the domesticated horse and mule had to adjust to a new environment and new ways. Equines were moved long distances on foot and by train and boat. They were branded "US" by Federal forces, and those owned by the Confederacy "CS."

Horses and mules are herd animals that flee when they perceive danger, and this tendency is not easy to overcome. Equines had to be trained to tolerate various noises, including that of a bugle, music, and gun. Many never adjusted. An example is the mule, which became uncontrollable around cannon fire. The best horses were selected for artillery work and had to tolerate the thunderous roar of artillery firing a few feet away. Horses never ridden had to be broken, which involved violent bucking and kicking. The rider frequently launched in the air and often sustained an injury from the impact of hitting the unwelcoming ground. The horse's and mule's back feet could be lethal weapons, often inflicting injury that was sometimes fatal. Mules had to get used to large packs stacked on their backs and, like the horse, pull wagons.

Pack mule (John D. Billings, *Hardtack and Coffee*)

(John D. Billings, *Hardtack and Coffee*)

The cavalry horse and rider had to learn maneuvers spelled out in "Poinsett's Tactics" (1841), also known as the "41 Tactics" by former US Secretary of War J. R. Poinsett. Later in the war, they followed the exquisitely detailed instructions in *The 1862 U.S. Cavalry Tactics* by Union cavalry Officer Philip St. George Cooke. The latter provided comprehensive instructions from training and riding a horse to manuals of arms for swords and pistols, over 200 maneuvers, and music for all 38 bugle calls. It even had instructions on using a saber against a lance, unsuited for use in wooded terrain. The lance was used only by the 6th Pennsylvania Cavalry Regiment early in the war and was soon exchanged for the carbine. Few mastered the contents of Cooke's textbook. Most learned to be cavalrymen from experiences on the battlefield.

Before the war, it was believed it took three years to train cavalrymen. Once the war started, it was considered six months, but the experiences during the war made leadership soon realize it took more than a year. Union Captain Charles Rhodes maintained it was common knowledge in the cavalry "that a cavalryman was of little value until he had had two years of service."[57]

The need for training was greater for the Union than for the Confederates, who generally grew up riding horses and understood how to ride and care for them. The horses in the North were primarily pulling carriages in the city and on the farm; muscular draft animals like Percherons or Clydesdales and other powerful breeds pulled plows and heavily loaded wagons. Draft horses replaced the strong but slower oxen that dominated farm work into the 1800s. The draft horse could pull a plow at twice the speed of an ox. But their size and weight made them too slow and unsuited for cavalry work. Horses are known to run 27 to 40 miles per hour, but the draft horse can only lumber along at half of that speed at ten to 15 miles per hour.

---

57   Philip St. Geo. Cooke, *The 1862 U. S. Cavalry Tactics* (Mechanicsburg, PA: Stackpole Books, 2004), 27-44.

Many new cavalry recruits needed to learn how to care for their mount, including properly adjusting the blanket under the saddle, what to feed, knowing when to limit the amount of water their horse drank after a long ride and during stops, and unloosening the saddle to prevent a debilitating sore back for his mount. In addition, recruits had to learn and maintain proper posture when riding straight in the saddle. Sitting to one side, slouching, and swinging lead to a sore back for the animal. They had to learn to limit what the horse had to carry in addition to the rider. But there was a paramount rule after a ride troopers had to heed: always take care of your horse before yourself. Failure to take proper care of the equines was the leading cause of disability and mortality of horses and mules during the Civil War. Although negligence was a crucial factor in the troopers' maltreatment of his mount, sometimes, it was unintentional due to incompetence and lack of knowledge and skill.

In Union cavalry camps early in the war were lopped-eared horses, the result of saber drills during which the trooper's failure to control their sabers led to him accidentally cutting off the horse's ear. While performing saber drills, soldiers also injured themselves by breaking their wrists after unintentionally striking a tree limb. This led to sabers being called "wrist breakers."[58]

Until the beginning of the third year of the war, Union cavalry recruits struggled to master what was needed to be effective cavalrymen. An example typical of their first experiences was graphically told by Captain George Vanderbilt of the 10th New York Cavalry. The men had been in service for about a month, and in December of 1862, they were going on their first escort movement. They burdened their mounts with numerous extra cartridges, large quilts made by

---

58 Miller, *The Photographic History of the Civil War*, 25, 29, 48, 60-62. Armistead, *Horses and Mules in the Civil War*, 34. "Draft Horse," Wikipedia, https:en.wikipedia.org>wiki>Draft_horse.

their mothers, frying pans, and coffee pots. When they attempted to follow the general leading them, bedlam occurred:

> Such a rattling, jingling, jerking, scrabbling, cursing, I never heard before. Green horses—some of them had never been ridden—turned round and round, backed against each other, jumped up or stood up like trained circus horses. Some of the boys had a pile in front on their saddles, and one in the rear, so high and heavy it took two men to saddle one horse and two men to help the fellow into his place. The horses sheered out, going sideways, pushing the well-disposed animals out of position, etc. Some of the boys had never ridden anything since they galloped on a hobby horse, and they clasped their legs close together, thus unconsciously sticking the spurs into the horses' sides.

This was the crowd Vanderbilt was in charge of, and he ordered his men to follow their general. They started over again, and the general "went like greased lightning."

> In less than ten minutes Tenth New York cavalrymen might have been seen on every hill for two miles rearward. Poor fellows! I wanted to help them, but the general was 'On to Richmond,' and I hardly looked back for fear of losing them . . . It was my first Virginia ride as a warrior in the field . . . I was wondering what in the mischief I should say when we halted and none of the company was there but me . . . Blankets slipped from under the saddles and hung from one corner; saddles slipped back until they were on the rump of horses; others turned and were on the underside of animals; horses running and kicking; tin pans, mess-kettkes, patent sheet-iron stoves the boys had seen in illustrated papers and sold by sutlers of Alexandria—about as useful as a piano or folding bed—flying through the air; and all I could do was to give a hasty glance to the rear and sing out at the top of my

voice, 'C-l-o-s-e u-p!' But they couldn't 'close.' Poor boys! Their eyes stuck out like those of maniacs. We went only a few miles, but the boys didn't all get up till noon.[59]

Union Secretary of War Edwin M. Stanton's order four months earlier was not followed. It was to prevent the above from occurring. Stanton decreed that before anyone could be mustered into the cavalry service, the mustering officer must give each candidate an examination testing their horsemanship, "and no person shall be mustered into cavalry service who does not exhibit good horsemanship and practical knowledge of the ordinary care and treatment of horses."[60]

Mustering officers frequently gave the examination, which was inadequate to test a recruit's knowledge of caring for a horse. A Union cavalryman recalls recruits for the 5th Michigan being mounted on a horse without a saddle and trotting around in a circle. If they stayed on the horse and did not fall off, they passed and were accepted into service.

Soldiers preferred the cavalry over being on foot, which entailed marching long distances while carrying a rifle-musket, accouterments, ammunition, and a bedroll and canteen, among other items. When John Mosby formed his Rangers, men joined him on raids, hoping to capture a horse from the enemy so they could become cavalrymen. Although they were on the same side, the relationship between foot soldiers and troopers was often not friendly and led to verbal sparring. When the cavalry was pulled back at the start of a battle, those riding might hear a soldier shout, "There must be a battle coming because the cavalry is going to the rear." Confederate infantryman J. B. Polley wrote his wife, "About the strongest feeling

---

[59] Miller, *The Photographic History of the Civil War*, 26, 28, 30.
[60] OR, Ser. III, 380.

infantry and cavalry have for each other is that of contempt." The cavalrymen thought they were superior to foot soldiers, who felt the cavalry did not do their share of fighting. One of Polley's comrades verbalized this by saying cavalrymen never got close enough to Yankees to be killed.[61]

THE FORTUNES OF CONFEDERATE CAVALRY WANE

Most of the Confederate cavalry came from eight states: Virginia, Kentucky, Missouri, Tennessee, Texas, Alabama, Mississippi, and South Carolina. There were 104 Confederate generals who led Southern cavalry. Most of them were capable and effective leaders. But their effectiveness waned as the size of the Confederacy shrunk along with diminishing resources, including horses, which were far less than those of the Union from the start. Until the middle of 1863, Confederate cavalry dominated that of the Union. The following are several examples.

In 1862, the flamboyant Jeb Stuart rode twice around George McClellan's army during the Peninsular and Antietam Campaigns, which was more show than damage to the enemy. Much smaller in scale but equally embarrassing to the Union was John S. Mosby's daring night raid early in 1863 upon a Union camp at Fairfax Courthouse behind Union lines in Northern Virginia, where Mosby captured slumbering Union General Edwin Stoughton and Union horses. Lincoln wryly remarked that he did not mind losing a general as much as he did the horses: "I can make a better general in five minutes, but the horses cost a hundred and twenty-five dollars apiece."[62] In late 1862, Jeb Stuart made four successful raids to harass General Ambrose Burnside's Union forces north of Fredericksburg

---

61 Armistead, *Horse and Mules in the Civil War*, 33.
62 James A. Ramage, *Gray Ghost*, Lexington: University Press of Kentucky, 71. Bennett H. Young, *Confederate Wizards of the Saddle*, Boston: Chapple Publishing Company, 1914), xviii, xx.

and strike his supply bases. Stuart captured men, horses, wagons, mules, and supplies. The day after Christmas, he started the last raid, Stuart's Dumfries Raid, routing Union forces sent after him and going within 12 miles of Washington, D.C., capturing a telegraph station and wiring a message to Union Quartermaster General Montgomery Meigs complaining about the "bad quality of the mules lately furnished" to the raiders.

The Gettysburg campaign in mid-1863 revealed the Union cavalry coming of age and the Confederate loss of supremacy. This became apparent at Brandy Station, Virginia, on June 9th, 1863, where over 20,000 men (Union forces had slightly greater numbers) clashed sabers in what was the largest cavalry battle in the Civil War and considered the greatest cavalry battle ever contested in North America. The action was a draw, despite the Federals withdrawing first from the battlefield. They left having destroyed the Confederate cavalry's invincibility. As Lee moved northward west of the Blue Ridge Mountains, Confederate cavalry east of the mountains under Jeb Stuart was shoved toward the Blue Ridge in the bloodiest small cavalry battles of the war at Aldie, Middleburg, and Upperville, Virginia. However, Stuart successfully delayed Federal cavalry from reaching the mountain gaps until Lee had moved safely northward. Stuart then moved eastward, crossing the Potomac behind the Union Army, and did not arrive at Gettysburg until the second day of the battle. On the third day, northeast of the main battlefield, he was defeated by Union cavalry.

Although Union cavalry was becoming dominant, it was far from perfect. As Stuart's cavalry was being defeated, the bold Union cavalry leader General Hugh Judson Kilpatrick sent cavalry under General Elon John Farnsworth on a senseless and doomed charge over uneven terrain against an enemy behind stone fences in the southern part of the main Gettysburg battlefield. The charge was one of the most disastrous of the war. Farnsworth received five mortal wounds, 66 of his men were killed, and many were wounded and captured. Kilpatrick's nickname, "Kil-Cavalry" was well earned; the result of reckless fighting and the lack of concern for his men were reflected in his poor judgment in ordering the Farnsworth attack at Gettysburg and later in the war in the Kilpatrick-Dahlgren raid on Richmond.[63]

Eighteen sixty-three saw the Confederate cavalry diminish in effectiveness along with the rest of the Confederate Army. Gettysburg and Vicksburg were turning points. They were monumental Confederate defeats that culminated within a day of each other. The three-day Battle of Gettysburg was over on July 3rd, and Grant's eight-month campaign to capture Vicksburg occurred on July 4th. Lee no longer had the offensive power he had before Gettysburg. With the fall of Vicksburg, the Confederacy was split and separated by the Union's control of the Mississippi River. The Union cavalry played a significant role. Union General Benjamin Grierson's raid into Louisiana successfully diverted attention from Grant, crossing the Mississippi River eastward and leading to the capture of Vicksburg.

After Gettysburg, Confederate leaders were aware of their loss of cavalry supremacy. It had been rapid. The extensive cavalry combat during the Gettysburg campaign, declining resources, and the Federals finally becoming organized had taken a heavy toll on Southern horsemen. Two months after Gettysburg, Colonel John R. Chambliss, Jr. of the Army of Northern Virginia was ordered to find out "the causes of the present condition of the cavalry that have produced the difference which now exists between its present condition

---

63   Mark M. Boatner III, *The Civil War Dictionary*, (New York: David McKay Company, 1959), 339, 460-461. Edward G. Longacre, *The Cavalry at Gettysburg* (London: Associated University Press, 1986), 244.

than that of a few months ago." His report was ominous: "A great disparity exists between the effective cavalry force of the enemy and ours." Chambliss gave an extensive list of how the Southern cavalry was inferior to that of the Union. These included inferior weapons, ammunition, and "miserably inferior sabers." Chambliss stressed that a solution was needed for the acute shortage of veterinarians and hospitals for horses. Causing the most dissatisfaction and disorganization in the cavalry was the inability to get a horse, which led to the repeated chorus:

> When am I to get another horse, and how can I buy one at the present prices after I have lost so many without compensation from the Government? I know that a majority of my most efficient men have lost one to five horses broken down by hardships of service, and a small minority of horses lost in service are killed in battle . . . The chief cause of the present dismembered and shattered state of our ranks has been the want of horseshoes and horseshoe nails, forges and transportation.

Providing "every soldier with shoe pouches, and shoes to put in them" would lead to fewer dismounted men. "During the late exposition into the enemy's country many valuable horses were lost due to the want of shoes."[64]

Despite the waning fortunes of the Confederacy in 1863, the war would last two more years, running the total for military actions from battles and campaigns to minor skirmishes and scouting, not counting naval activity, to 10,455. The horse and mule were vital, from draft animals to carrying troopers and partisans into combat and on long, exhausting raids. In 1864, Confederates had some successful encounters with the enemy, like Jeb Stuart's Chambersburg,

---

64   OR, Ser. IV, vol 2, 718-721.

Pennsylvania, raid and Wade Hampton's victory in Virginia at Trevilian Station that stopped Union General Philip Sheridan from cutting the Virginia Central Railroad, which was Robert E. Lee's essential supply line.

At Yellow Tavern outside of Richmond, outnumbered Stuart unsuccessfully attempted to block Philip Sheridan's raid on the Confederate capital and lost his life. Farther west, success also eluded Confederate General Sterling Price, whose raid into Missouri failed to recover that state for the Confederacy.[65]

Some prominent cavalry leaders, Nathan B. Forrest and John S. Mosby, lacked military training. They were among the exceptions. Most top Union and Confederate cavalry leaders had some military training before the war. The majority of those leading the Federal cavalry had attended West Point. Forrest had only six months of formal education and never lost a battle until the end of the war. His raids so aggravated Union General William Tecumseh Sherman that he put Forrest at the top of his hit list. The exasperated Union commander stated, "That devil Forrest must be hunted down and killed if it costs ten thousand lives and bankrupts the Federal treasury."[66] In northern Virginia, attorney Mosby, from 1863 to 1865, expanded his Rangers from a couple of dozen to around 300, resulting in 700 men who served under his command. He harassed Union forces with swift and elusive raids, earning him the nickname "Gray Ghost." Devoid of civilian county government in the latter years of the war in Loudoun and Fauquier counties in Virginia, Mosby controlled this area, which began to be called "Mosby's Confederacy" as the Union made weekly forays into the region in an attempt to get

---

65   Boatner, *The Civil War Dictionary*, 669, 814, 848. Wikipedia, "Battle of Yellow Tavern," https://en.wikipedia.org>wiki>Battle_of_Yellow_Ta. The Battle of Trevilian Station was fought solely by cavalry, making it one of the largest cavalry battles during the war. The Battle of Brandy Station was larger.
66   Boatner, *The Civil War Dictionary*, 289.

rid of the 125-pound Confederate colonel and his Rangers that tied up Union men needed elsewhere. Generals Lee and Jeb Stuart considered Mosby a valuable scout. Mosby and his men captured over 3,500 horses and mules.[67] For Forrest and Mosby, creativity trumped military training.

By contrast, Union General George Stoneman, who graduated from the military academy and was a classmate of George McClellan, was so ineffective as chief of cavalry in a raid during the Chancellorsville Campaign in 1863 that he was replaced by General Alfred Pleasonton and transferred to the west. During a raid in the Atlanta Campaign in 1864 to free prisoners at Andersonville, Stoneman's poor judgment led to his and 700 of his men's capture.[68]

During the Civil War, the cavalry played six significant roles: surveillance, screening, flank security, attacks, headquarters duties, and raiding. There were numerous raids during the Civil War. The most attention-getting were long-distance raids, but critics question their value despite the fame, arguing they were often of little strategic importance compared to the lost men and horses. Jeb Stuart's third attempt to ride around the Army of the Potomac severely hurt Lee's chances for victory at Gettysburg. Stoneman's raid in the Chancellorsville battle was labeled a failure despite destroying Confederate property because he lost 1,000 horses, ruined by overexertion, and men and equipment as well. The most successful long raid was Grierson's Raid in the Vicksburg campaign, considered a strategic masterpiece drawing vital Confederate forces away from Grant's Union Army.

---

67   Ramage, *Gray Ghost*, 346. Major John Scott, *Partisan Life with Col. John S. Mosby* (New York: Harpers & Brothers, 1869), 476. By the war's end, of Mosby's 700 men, 100 were in Union prisons.
68   Boatner, *The Civil War Dictionary*, 501-503.

Long raids, success or failure, took a heavy toll on both the rider and his mount by exceeding the capacity of the significant mobility horses gave the cavalry. A horse could travel 35 miles in eight hours without fatiguing the horse or rider. Some raids far exceeded this. During Jeb Stuart's Chambersburg Raid in 1862, his men covered 80 miles in 27 hours, and in one of John Hunt Morgan's raids into Kentucky, Tennessee, and Ohio in 1862 and 1863, his troopers averaged 21 hours in the saddle. On one occasion, Morgan went 95 miles in 35 hours. The horse had to carry the rider's weight in addition to the weight of his weapons, blanket, canteen, sundry, and other items, which increased the mount's burden on long raids. Confederate General "Fighting Joe" Wheeler's raid in 1864 during the Atlanta Campaign was 36 days, and Sterling Price's raid into Missouri lasted 97 days and covered 1,439 miles. The need for replacement horses on long raids led Jeb Stuart to seize 1,000 horses in Pennsylvania from farmers and townspeople, many unbroken and some heavy workhorses unsuited for cavalry, hindering Confederates during the cavalry battle on the third day at Gettysburg.[69]

EVOLUTION OF WEAPONS

Several significant changes before and during the Civil War increased the destructiveness of weapons. Two of the most important were the development of the rifle-musket and the conical-shaped bullet called the Minié ball. The primary weapon in earlier wars was the smoothbore musket with an effective range between 50 to 100 yards. Its range was so limited General Grant, commenting on this, is to have said with some exaggeration, "A man could shoot at you all day, from 150 yards, and you would not notice it."

---

69 Boatner, *The Civil War Dictionary*, 67-71. Wikipedia, "Price's Missouri Expedition," http://en.wikipedia.org>wiki> _Missouri_Exped. Ezra J. Warner, *Generals in Blue* (Baton Rouge: Louisiana State Press, 1981), 481-482. Wikipedia, "Cavalry in the American Civil War," https://en.wikipedia.org>wiki>cavalry_in_the_Americ.

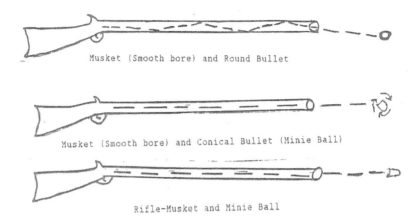

   The spiral lines in the barrel of a rifle-musket and the conical-shaped bullet with a cavity at its base had an effective range of 200 to 300 yards and did harm over 1,000 yards. The conical-shaped bullet is more accurate than the round ball. It is smaller than the rifle bore and more easily dropped down it. Upon firing, the skirt around the bullet's hollow base expands to the bore, trapping the gas from the exploded powder and sending the spiraling projectile much farther than the round ball due to the lines, or rifling, in the barrel.[70]

   The rifle-musket's range eliminated the traditional cavalry charge on infantry and forced artillery away from the enemy to get out of its range. Cavalry and infantry charges had to be made from longer distances and endure more enemy fire and casualties. Antoine-Henri Jomini, one of the founders of modern military thought, advocated the theory of the superiority of offense over defense. Before the rifle-musket, artillery could be much closer and fire upon the enemy, followed by an infantry or cavalry charge. This

---

70   William B. Edwards, *Civil War Guns*, (Harrisburg, Pennsylvania: The Stackpole Company, 1962), 15-17, 159. Francis A. Lord, *Civil War Collector's Encyclopedia* (New York: Castle Books, 1965), 253.

tactic applied against soldiers armed with the rifle-musket was far less successful and more deadly.

An example is Pickett's third-day, hour-long charge at Gettysburg across nearly a mile of open field that temporarily penetrated part of the Union line before being forced to retreat, sustaining over 50 percent casualties of the 12,000 Confederates. Horses were too valuable to lose charging foot soldiers armed with rifle-muskets. Only battles between cavalry were fought on horseback. Dismounted cavalrymen became more important in combat as the war progressed. The rifle-musket was the principal weapon killer in the Civil War, inflicting far more casualties than any other weapon. It was responsible for four-fifths or more of all battle casualties, some estimating it to be as high as 92 percent. Popular models were the M1855 rifle-musket, the 1855 Harpers Ferry rifle-musket, the Springfield rifle-musket (also known as the US rifle of 1861), and the Enfield the Union and Confederates imported from England. The Confederates also depended on the weapons taken from the Union on the battlefields.

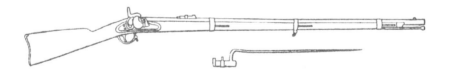

M1855 rifle-musket (*The Official Military Atlas of the Civil War*)

A soldier uses a ramrod, which is inserted into the barrel of a musket or rifle-musket to compress the bullet and powder together at the base of the barrel. (Alexander Hunter, *Johnny Reb and Billy Yank*)

Three hundred seventy different types of small arms with 56 calibers ranging from .22 to .858 were used in the Civil War. The Union used 90,000,000 pounds of lead and 26,000,000 pounds of powder. Many of the shots fired in combat did not hit the target. It is estimated that to kill one man, it took 900 pounds of lead and 240 pounds of powder. Over 10,000,000 Civil War bullets have been excavated, only half of which had been fired. The cavalry on both sides were armed with three weapons: the saber, carbine, and pistol. However, early in the war, the Union cavalry was inferiorly armed to the Confederates. By 1862, most Union troopers had sabers and pistols, but few had carbines until 1863. A few men on both sides carried eight-foot lances that were soon discarded because of their impracticality. Southerner cavalrymen brought their shotguns with them early in the war, effective only at close range and later replaced with carbines. Some partisan cavalry used double-barrel shotguns at close range instead of pistols. Pistols, six-shot Colt, and Remington revolvers were carried by cavalry on both sides. The revolver was John S. Mosby's weapon of choice. He had four: two in his holster and two in his saddle bags. Swords were frequently used in clashes between cavalries. Almost 400,000 light and heavy sabers were purchased by the Union during the war. These were superior in quality to the cheaper swords issued to Southern cavalrymen. The carbines were short, light, and had repeating firepower, such as the famous seven-shot Spencer, Henry, and Sharps carbines. They were more available to Union than Southern horsemen, putting them and their foot soldiers with single-shot rifle-muskets at a significant disadvantage. It took an average of 30 seconds to load and reload a rifle-musket, with the most experienced soldier firing two to three shots per minute. In the meantime, the seven-shot Spencer rifle could get off a shot every three to four seconds that could penetrate through 13 inches of wood at 150 feet and throw a projectile with a degree of accuracy over one mile. Late in the war, the Union cavalry had the 16-shot Henry carbine (repeater). Confederates lamented, "That damn Yankee rifle." The Yankees are not fair; they have guns they "load up on Sunday and shot all the rest of the week."[71]

Union General "Little Phil" Sheridan was the most innovative Civil War general in using the carbine to create a mounted cavalry that became the equal of the infantry and artillery. His mounted and dismounted cavalry played a significant role in taking offensive

---

71   William B. Edwards, *Civil War Guns*, (Harrisburg, Pennsylvania: The Stackpole Company, 1962), 15-17, 159. Francis A. Lord, *Civil War Collector's Encyclopedia* (New York: Castle Books, 1965), 253.

action in 1864 in the Winchester and Cedar Creek battles in the Shenandoah Campaign of 1864.[72]

Sabers and bayonets inflicted few casualties. Of the 275,174 wounded and 110,100 Union killed in combat, the saber and bayonet were responsible for 922 wounds and 56 fatalities.

---

[72] Ivan G. Hoss, *Weapons of the Civil War* (New York: Military Press, 1987), 8-29. Jeffry D. Wert, *From Winchester to Ceda* (Carlisle, PA: South Mountain Press, 1987). 24 Wikipedia. "Cavalry in the American Civil War." https://en.wikipedia.org>wiki>Cavalry in the Americ. When cavalrymen fought dismounted, men were assigned to hold the horses behind the battle.

CHAPTER 4

EQUINE CELEBRITIES

Most of the thousands of horses, like thousands of men who fought in the Civil War, are unknown. Only a few of both are well known. The anonymous human participants' names are recorded in archives, but the horses' names are not. After all, some would say they were not humans and were too numerous to record. Due to the extensive research of Gene C. Armistead, we do have a roster of more than 700 war horses. A number were named after someone the owner admired, but most were given random names, like the most used name, Billy, and even more had Old preceding their name, like Old Tom. The most unusual name was Sardanapalus, after ancient Assyria's last king; the least flattering was Pug Ugly. The best-known Civil War horses are those of famous Civil War leaders. The famous mounts of the war derive fame from being associated with their celebrity rider. Two of the most renowned mounts, Traveller and Fancy (Little Sorrel), were ridden by two of the most famous figures of the war: Robert E. Lee and Stonewall Jackson, respectively.

Traveller is the most famous horse in the Civil War and has been called the most famous in history, but he was not Lee's only mount. In the spring of 1861, the citizens of Richmond gave Lee a horse named Richmond. Richmond was a fine-looking horse but lacked stamina and easily fatigued. He was nervous around strange horses and prone to squeal and buck. Richmond died in the summer of 1862 after being ridden in hot weather and being bled when he was slow to recover. Bloodletting was a medical practice going back to colonial America based on removing impure fluids believed to cause illness. Earlier that spring, Lee purchased another horse called The Roan or Brown-Roan. During the spring of 1862, during the Seven Days' Battles, The Roan started going blind and died at Malvern Hill. After the Second Battle of Bull Run, Jeb Stuart gave Lee a quiet mare called Lucy Long to spell Traveller. She was sparely ridden until the Appomattox Campaign when she disappeared. She was rediscovered shortly after the war, and Lee, in memory of Jeb Stuart, purchased her from her bogus owner. Lucy Long became the mount for Lee's daughters until declining health led to her life of 33 years ending by being chloroformed. After the Second Battle of Bull Run, Lee was given another horse called Ajax. Ajax was too tall for Lee and was rarely ridden by the Confederate commander. But none of these equines were as pleasing to Lee as Traveller.[73]

Previous owners called him Jeff Davis and Greenbrier. After purchasing the iron-gray horse for $200, which he first saw in Greenbrier County, Virginia (now West Virginia), Lee changed his name to Traveller (with two Ls). He liked Traveller's gait and rode Traveller throughout the war. Others found Traveller's bouncy gait uncomfortable and fatiguing. Lee's son, Robert E. Lee Jr., verified this:

---

73   George Worthington Adams, *Doctors in Blue,* (New York: Collier Books, 1961), 110. Armistead, *Horses and Mules in the Civil War*, 109. 141. 167, 177-180. Boatner, *The Civil War Dictionary*, 478. J. D. R. Hawkins, *Horses in Gray*, (Gretna: Pelican Publishing Company, 2017), 48-49. 106-107. Charles G. Worman, *Civil War Animals*, (Lynchburg, VA: Schroder Publications, 1011), 198.

During my soldier life, so far, I had been on foot, having nothing more lively than tired artillery horse, so I mounted with some misgivings, though I was proud of my steed. My misgivings were fully realized, for Traveller would not walk a step. He took a short, high trot—a buck-trot, as compared with a kick-jump—and kept it up to Fredericksburg, some thirty miles. Though young and strong, and tough, I was glad when the journey ended. I think I am safe saying that I could have walked the distance with much less discomfort and fatigue.[74]

Traveller's flightiness inadvertently saved both Lee and his silver-gray gelding from injury or death during the Battle of Spotsylvania. Traveller reared upon hearing the thunderous roar of cannon fire as a cannon ball passed under his belly. After the weary war years ended, Traveller accompanied the defeated Confederate commander to Lexington, Virginia, where Lee became the president of Washington College (now Washington and Lee University). The highlight of the day for Lee at Lexington was his evening rides on Traveller through the neighborhood, often giving local kids a piggyback ride. Traveller was a celebrity to the community, and if given the rare opportunity, his admirers picked hairs from the war horse's mane and tail as one young man did when Lee was away, filling his pockets with the horse's hair. When Lee died in 1870, Traveller was part of the funeral possession. Two years later, Traveller died from lockjaw due to stepping on a nail. He was buried on the college campus. It was a gloomy occasion, and not a word was spoken. Lee's son, Custis, oversaw the burial as four young girls watched and three black men dug a large hole in the red clay. The bottom was covered with wood (which later deteriorated), the carcass covered with lime to reduce the smell of decaying flesh, wood was attached to the floorboards, and a wooden top was added. Later, Traveller's bones

---

[74] Worman, *Civil War Animals*, 149-150.

were sent to Rochester, New York, in the mid-1870s for bleaching, and some argue that they should be displayed in a museum. The bleaching failed to remove the stains from the red clay, which was prominent where the horse had been buried. In 1907, the bones were mounted and displayed in the Washington College museum, where students carved their initials into the bones for good luck. This, along with deterioration, resulted in the bones being reinterred in a large wooden box on the college campus in 1971.[75]

GENERAL LEE ON TRAVELER

(Gamaliel Bradford, Jr., *Lee the American*)

The second most famous horse in the Civil War was called Fancy by Stonewall Jackson and Little Sorrel by others. Jackson became as attached to Fancy as Lee was to Traveller. He got Fancy in 1861 at Harpers Ferry when his forces seized several horses from a Union supply train. Jackson took two horses: Big Sorrel, a large

---

75 Armistead, *Horse and Mules in The Civil War,* 180. Hawkins, *Horses in Gray,* 38-41. Worman, *Civil War Animals,* 148, 151-152.

stallion, and a small gelding for his wife, whom he called Fancy. The former Virginia Military Institute (VMI) instructor soon found Big Sorrel, flighty and gun-shy, difficult to control. Jackson, by contrast, was pleased with Fancy's easy gait and pleasant disposition and kept him. Fancy was a Morgan horse, had stamina to carry Stonewall 40 miles at a time, and a smooth gait that allowed Jackson to fall asleep in the saddle on long marches. Fancy amused his owner by the way he slept lying on the ground like a dog. While awake, he would roll over with his feet up in the air. Jackson, like Lee, was highly fond of his mounts. Jackson frequently fed Fancy apples. The pair did not make a striking appearance, with the rider usually wearing a well-worn uniform, a cap pulled down near his nose, and stirrups too short that put the rider's knees level with the horse's back. Jackson was not a graceful rider, and he leaned forward when he rode because his uncle had trained him to be a jockey.

Appearance aside, both Jackson and Fancy became icons. Fancy carried Jackson through the war until Stonewall's fatal wounding, except for a brief period during the Antietam Campaign when Fancy was lost or stolen. The celebrity of Fancy, whom Jackson's men had called Little Sorrel, continued after the war. Fancy stayed with Jackson's widow until her age led her to give the famous horse to VMI. After several years, Fancy, now frequently called Old Sorrel, was moved to the Confederate Soldiers' Home in Richmond. Fancy's popularity did not wane as he was shipped by train and put on display at Confederate veterans' reunions, fairs, and the World's Fair in New Orleans in 1885. The previous year, when put on display at the Maryland State Fair in Hagerstown, veterans crowded around Fancy, telling their children about the famous gelding. With grabbing fingers, many admirers pulled handfuls of hair from his mane and tail to have a memento of the celebrity horse. J. D. R. Hawkins wrote of the result: "Little Sorrel was nearly plucked clean." Southern ladies also took his hair to make bracelets and rings as souvenirs. Fancy died at 33 in 1886, having lived longer than the average age of a horse, which was between 25 and 30 years. His hide was removed and stretched over a plaster of paris frame. Fancy's mounted remains were displayed in the Confederate Soldiers' Home in Richmond, Virginia, until 1949, when it was sent to VMI, where it resides today in the institution's museum.[76]

Fancy (Little Sorrel) in 1863, shortly after the death of Jackson (Library of Congress)

Other horses, usually those of prominent officers on both sides, became well known during the war, but their fame was not

---

76   Armistead, *Horses and Mules in the Civil War*, 130-132. J. D. R. Hawkins, *Horses in Gray*, 52-67. Worman, *Civil War Animal Heroes*, 172-179. The skeleton of Fancy was given to the taxidermist Frederick Webster, who reconstructed the skeleton and, in 1903, gave it to the Carnegie Institute, which caused cries the skeleton should remain in the South. In 1949, it was sent to where it remained on display in a biology classroom for 40 years until the bones were boxed up and stored.

as widespread or lasting as Traveller's and Fancy's. This group included General U. S. Grant's Cincinnati and Jeff Davis, General George Meade's Old Baldy, General Philip Sheridan's Rienzi, and Confederate Turner Ashby's Tom Telegraph.

Cincinnati was the son of Lexington, whom many considered the fastest Thoroughbred in the United States, and was a large horse, nearly six feet tall (7.5 hands), that Grant claimed was "the finest horse that I have ever seen." Grant protected Cincinnati and only allowed a few people to ride him. Grant's second favorite was a much smaller horse, Jeff Davis, captured in a cavalry raid on Joe Davis' plantation near Vicksburg. Joe was the brother of Jefferson Davis, the president of the Confederacy. An outstanding Canadian Pacer horse sired Jeff Davis. His gait made for easy riding, and he was often ridden by Grant on long trips.[77]

General Grant's mounts: Cincinnati (left) and Jeff Davis (right) in 1864. Note the difference in the size of the two horses. (The Library of Congress)

---

[77] Armistead, *Horses and Mules of the Civil War*, 125, 143. Worman, *Civil War Animal Heroes*, 202-206. A hand is four inches. One of the other horses Grant had was named Egypt. He was ridden in the last part of the war.

Horses often received multi-battle wounds, frequently not surviving; one that did was General George Meade's bullet-scarred Baldy. Wounded twice at the First Battle of Bull Run, after a deep neck wound at Antietam, he was left for dead and later found quietly grazing. At Gettysburg, an enemy bullet lodged between his ribs, and he was wounded again at Weldon Station in the Petersburg Campaign in August 1864, ending his participation in the war. Baldy followed Meade's hearse to the cemetery, surviving his former owner by ten years. Two Civil War veterans exhumed Baldy's remains and cut off his head and front hooves in memory of the general. The mounted head of Baldy is displayed at the Grand Army of the Republic Civil War Museum & Library in Philadelphia.[78]

Baldy in 1863 (Library of Congress)

---

78 Armistead, *Horses and Mules in the Civil War*, 110-111. Miller, *The Photographic History of The Civil War*, 295. Meade got Baldy after the First Battle of Bull Run.

The fame of Tom Telegraph and his owner, Confederate General Turner Ashby, who, as his biographer stated, "was one of the most accomplished horseback riders in either army," shone brightly in the early part of the war. Ashby selected his mounts based on their durability and speed. He chose two high-spirited, outstanding horses: a milk-white stallion and a coal-black stallion that was similar in build but differed only in color. Turner selected the white horse, Tom Telegraph, as his primary mount despite most cavalrymen shying away from a horse of that color because it made them stand out to the enemy as a target. The black stallion was his backup despite being unmanageable for everyone but Ashby. Stonewall Jackson depended heavily upon his cavalry leader, Turner Ashby, who performed admirably during the 1862 Valley Campaign in the Shenandoah Valley of Virginia. A significant part of his success was due to his white mount, who got him out of difficult situations. After being captured, Ashby was allowed to ride ahead of his captors; suddenly, Tom Telegraph wheeled to one side, jumping over the fence bordering the road and across a field to safety, leaving the startled enemy. Unfortunately, in the summer of 1862, neither horse nor rider would escape life-taking bullets. In April, Federals closed in on Ashby as he attempted to burn a bridge near New Market, Virginia. He could not accomplish this because the enemy was close and firing at him. One shot grazed Ashby's leg, going into the side of Tom Telegraph. Ashby's main force, farther away, anxiously watched as his white horse emerged from the bridge, followed by the few men who were with him, sweeping over the land until they reached safety over a mile away. The white stallion, covered in foam from heat and exertion, then collapsed, shot through the lungs, and suffered his last agony as he lay dying after carrying his rider to safety. Tom Telegraph had given his all. A sad Ashby bent over, stroked his mane, and looked into his dying horse's eyes. Later, Ashby's men plucked most of the hair from the famous steed's mane and tail for mementos. Less than two months later, outside of Harrisonburg, Virginia, the life of Tom Telegraph's rider ended when an enemy bullet penetrated his heart. Tom Telegraph and Turner Ashby's fame continued into the 1900s, but as time distanced the Civil War from later generations, their memory waned along with that of most Civil War horses and their riders.

Turner Ashby (Thomas Ashby, *Life of Turner Ashby*)

Union General Philip Sheridan's horse, Rienzi, also called Winchester, gained fame by rapidly traveling the 15 miles from Winchester, Virginia, to Cedar Creek Battlefield on October 19th, 1864. There, Sheridan rallied his forces, turning what had been a defeat into a victory. Poems were later written about the ride. Rienzi survived the war despite being wounded. Today, his body is on display at the Smithsonian Institution.[79]

Sheridan's horse Rienzi (Winchester) (Library of Congress)

---

79   Armistead, *Horses and Mules in the Civil War*, 167-169. Thomas A. Ashby, *The Life of Turner Ashby* (New York: Neale Publishing Company, 201-206. Henry Kyd Douglas, *I Rode With Stonewall* (Greenwood, Connecticut: Fawcett Publications, 1899), 49-50. Hawkins, *Horses in Gray*, 133-136.

During Sheridan's famous ride, Rienzi did not have all the trappings in this photograph.

Other horses of modest fame that faded with time were Mosby's favorite mount Dandy, McClellan's Daniel Webster, Medal of Honor winner Joshua L. Chamberlain's Charlemagne, Sherman's Lexington and Sam, the "Rock of Chickamauga" George H. Thomas' Billy, and Albert Sidney Johnston's Fire-Eater. Both Johnston and Fire-Eater were wounded in the Peach Orchard during the Battle of Shiloh in the spring of 1863. Fire-Eater was wounded four times. Johnston, ignoring the wound to his thigh, bled to death. Nathan Bedford Forrest's favorite mounts were Roderick and King Philip. King Philip was Forrest's only mount to survive the war.[80]

DANGERS OF HORSEMANSHIP

The war took a heavy toll on horses, celebrities and unknowns alike. The danger of riding a horse also existed. All riders had been thrown. An accident could happen during normal movement as well as perilous combat. The intrepid Confederate General Nathan Bedford Forrest was hard on horses. He killed 29 men and had 30 mounts shot from under him. He often stated he was "a horse ahead." During one battle, Forrest had four horses shot as he rode.[81] Early in the war, while engaging the enemy, Forrest's mount collided with two riderless horses, sending him flying 20 feet through the air before crashing to the ground and dislocating his shoulders. Later in the war, at Brice's Crossroads, Forrest's relentless pursuit of the enemy exhausted his men and himself in need of sleep. As they plodded forward, Forrest was asleep in the saddle, and his horse moved forward with his eyes closed, wandered off the road into a ditch, and hit

---

80 Cottrell, *Hoof Beats North and South*, 180.
81 Hawkins, *Horses in Gray*, 161. Worman, *Civil War Animal Heroes*, 68.

a tree, knocking the rider to the ground. Forrest lay there asleep for a while before he awoke.[82]

Robert E. Lee got hurt simply by standing by Traveller, holding the reins on the horse's neck. Shouts of "Yankee cavalry" led to hurried movement and a loud commotion, startling the horse. As Lee stepped forward to catch the reins, he tripped and fell, breaking a small bone in one hand and spraining the other. Both hands required splints.[83] General Ulysses Grant suffered a more severe injury during the Vicksburg Campaign when riding a horse he called "vicious and all but used." A locomotive frightened his mount, who fell on Grant, leaving him unconscious with a painful, swollen leg requiring more than a week's stay in a hotel and additional weeks of recuperating.[84] Stonewall Jackson met a similar fate when he got Fancy early in the war at Harpers Ferry. Thinking the new horse many called "Little Sorrel" was sluggish, Jackson used his spurs to urge her forward. She reared, throwing the rider to the ground and knocking him unconscious, causing days of suffering from a painful back injury.[85]

Officers and privates experienced varying degrees of injuries riding a horse, and parties on both sides perished. Confederate Brigadier General William Baldwin was killed when his stirrup broke, and Brigadier General Michael Corcoran was crushed to death when his horse fell on him.[86]

Many casualties were not due to horses or riders but the hazards of the environment, including uneven terrain or running into a tree limb. Riders' head injuries were the most prevalent, causing death and debilitating the rider from further service. *The Medical*

---

[82] Hawkins, *Horses In Gray*, 70, 80.
[83] Armistead, *Horses and Mules in the Civil War*, 37.
[84] U. S. Grant, *Personal Memoirs of U. S. Grant*, 580-581. Worman, *Civil War Animal Heroes*, 201-203.
[85] Worman, *Civil War Animal Heroes*, 175.
[86] No sources show how many of the Civil War's deaths were attributed to wild animals.

and Surgical History of the War of the Rebellion cites numerous examples. Private W. Alentharpe had to be discharged after being thrown from his horse and severely concussed. Private Frank Clune died after being thrown from his horse and falling violently upon his head. After rehabilitation, some returned to service, like Private Charles Sherman, who suffered from a severe concussion when thrown from his horse. After being treated, including being bled, he returned to service two months post injury.

Kicks from horses and mules were frequent causes of head injuries. George A. Tensdale suffered permanent vision impairment after being kicked by a horse. Less fortunate was a black teamster, Abraham, who died from a mule kick. Falls inflicting head injuries did not always involve animals. Henry Drimeyer was severely concussed after falling from a second-story window. C. S. Miller fell from a Harpers Ferry bridge and had to be discharged, and another man, John Miller, died after falling from a tree.

A variety of blows caused brain injuries. During combat, "they were commonly inflicted by clubbed muskets, falling tree limbs cut down by artillery, or kicks from horses and mules." Head injuries from private quarrels at camp or on the street "were more generally produced by blows from clubs or axes, slung shot [a heavy object attached to a strap] and various blunt objects, or bricks or stones."[87]

PRIDE IN HAVING A FAST, BEAUTIFUL MOUNT

The pride of the general and the average cavalryman was having a beautiful, fast mount. It was similar to the fixation in the 20th century in having a sleek, fast car. The pride of both led to betting and racing to see who had the most rapid. Egos got involved, which

---

[87] Joseph K. Barnes, *The Medical and Surgical History of the War of the Rebellion* (Washington: Government Printing Office, 1875), 40-47.

led to boasts, and bets were often made for more than they could afford. The issue was resolved by an impromptu race that commanding generals did not always approve. After the Battle of Wilson's Creek in 1861, Confederates who fought in the battle organized a horse race. Union General Thomas F. Meagher organized several steeplechase races to relax and distract his men before the Battle of Fair Oaks in 1862. Opposition from officers who opposed racing was because of the wear and tear on horses and gambling on races that hindered morale among the men who lost all their money. Since the colonial era, horse racing has been important in the North and especially in the South. The early racehorses were Quarter Horses, soon replaced with Thoroughbreds and Standardbreds (harness racers). Both civilians and men in the military were deeply involved in horse racing during the Civil War. The traditional view that horse racing vanished once the war started is incorrect. The need for horses for war curtailed horse racing in the South when the war began, but as it expanded in the North, it soon rebounded in the South. Danael Christian Suttle ably argues in his graduate thesis that "Racing was a mainstay during the Civil War." It was a diversion from the tedium of camp life and the horrors of combat and was important in maintaining morale. Suttle points out: "The war changed horse racing from a sport primarily enjoyed and operated by the wealthy to one influenced by the masses."[88]

---

[88] Danael Christian Suttle, "Horse Racing During the Civil War: The Perseverance of the Sport During a Time of National Crisis," Graduate Thesis, University of Arkansas, 2019. hhps://scholar-works.unark.edu/etd/3348/.

EQUINE CELEBRITIES

A desirable Union officer's mount (Library of Congress)

CHAPTER 5

A MIND OF THEIR OWN

Despite their position as underlings forced to bend to the will of their human handlers, mules and horses often violently protested against their plight. Although these behavior patterns are generally typical of horses and mules, each has its own personality, some deviating from what is considered typical for that species.

THE STUBBORN MULE

The top protester among horses and mules has to go to the indomitable mule. John Billings describes the temperamental nature of the mule as uncertain. One can never be sure how a mule will react. All sizes of mules, which vary in size more than horses, participated in the war. Kentucky, followed by Missouri, was the primary mule-producing state for the Union. The largest and best mules came from Kentucky; the smallest was a cross with a Mexican mustang. Regardless of size, the nervousness of mules and their intolerance of loud noises made them unfit for artillery and cavalry. Instead, their primary role was a draft animal, pulling ammunition, forage, and supply trains.

The mule also has advantages over a horse. They are tougher than horses and better able to withstand rugged use, lousy food, or no food, and neglect. When hay and grass were short, mule drivers cut and fed them branches. Mules would seek food, like most animals, on their own, like branches and bark. One mule ate his driver's overcoat. They are sure-footed and travel over rough terrain that would lame a horse.

They used various sizes of mules when organizing a six-mule team. Two larger mules beside a wagon with the wagon tongue between them are called pole mules. In the middle, a smaller pair called swing mules connected to the wagon tongue by single trees. Out front was an even smaller pair. If the wheel (pole) mules got stuck, those ahead could pull them out. Stout wheel mules served as a brake for frisky front mules. The mule driver rode a pole mule with a single rein in his left hand, which connected to the bit of the nearest-led mule. By pulling the left rein, the mules go left. One or more short jerks on the rein means to go right. The driver carried a black snake whip in his right hand. It was his instrument of discipline. A couple of loud snaps above their long, sensitive ears was accompanied by loud, lengthy shouts of profanity, which the driver believed was crucial to driving mules. Mules had a mind of their own and were not always docile. Mules were tricky and, out of the blue, could adopt an attitude, suddenly bracing their front feet and sitting down or throwing off the driver.[89]

---

89   John D. Billings, *Hardtack and Coffee*, (Pittsburg: P. J. Fleming & Co., 1888) 279-284, 289-293.

A SIX-MULE TEAM.

(John D. Billings, *Hardtack and Coffee*)

Back at camp, mules were usually attached to the pole (tongue)) of the wagon with three on each side. Billings described them as, "often as antic as kittens or puppies at play, leaping from one side of the pole to the other, lying down, tumbling over, and biting each other." But when pulling a wagon, they are in no mood to play. There, their behavior will be uncertain. Their primary weapon of protest is kicking, for which mules are known for worldwide. The mule that will not kick is unusual. After the Battle of Antietam, a black mule driver approached his unhitched mules. Suddenly, one kicked him, knocking him to the ground. In retaliation, the driver hit the mule on the head with a large stake, knocking it to the ground. The mule got up, shook its head, and according to Billings, the "driver and mule were at peace and understood each other." Bucking, along with biting and kicking, are displays of disgruntlement. Before the Battle of Antietam, a Confederate Army cook was riding a mule across the pontoon bridge at Harpers Ferry loaded with cooking pots and pans when suddenly the mule gave an ear-piercing bray and started kicking, throwing the rider and cooking ware into the Potomac River. The range and rapidity of a mule kick are far faster and greater than one would assume. Billings stated, "I have known [a mule] to kick a man 15 times in a second." On another occasion, Billings saw a driver knocked down with the mule's hind foot while "standing directly in front of him." He contended that the only way to control a mule was by grabbing or striking the mule's ears. In protest, when used as a pack animal with a vast pack hiding the animal except for his head and tail, when crossing a stream, he would lie down in the water, refusing to move. Nothing could be done until the load was taken off his back. The long-eared equines could severely impede the movement of an army by blocking traffic by squatting in the middle of a road. The propensity of mules to kick made putting shoes on them difficult. There were two ways: put him in a sling and strap his feet or walk him into a noose and tighten it around his legs, which caused him to struggle violently for a while. After the struggle, shoes were attached.[90]

Soldiers have remarked they can recall carcasses of horses along their line of march that died from exhaustion and disease but not dead mules. Billings wrote: "There are thousands of these men who would take a solemn oath that they never saw a dead mule during the war." One of the reasons for their fatalities being far fewer than that of horses was the mule's nature: endurance and aversion to the loud noise of combat, which they attempted to avoid. The sound of artillery could send them in any direction; they may go toward the enemy or back into their forces. During the Battle of Port Republic in 1862, upon hearing cannon fire, the mules just sat down in the middle of the battlefield. The following year, at Wauhatchie, Tennessee, about 200 mules were frightened by the noise of the battle during the night and ran into the Confederate lines of Wade Hampton, causing the Confederates to fall back, thinking they were under a cavalry attack.[91]

One of the Union raids of the war involved mules, referred to as the Lightning Mule Brigade, led by United States Army Colonel Abel D. Streight. He was ordered in the spring of 1863 to

---

[90] Ibid. 293-295.
[91] Armistead, *Horses and Mules the Civil War*, 72-81." Streight's Raid," Encyclopedia of Alabama, https://encylopedia of Alabama.org>streights-raid.

go into Alabama and destroy a portion of a railroad that supplied Confederates. Lacking horses, Streight got mules from farms in western Tennessee; many were unbroken, old, had sore backs, were weak, and had to have frequent breaks to rest. Confederates belittled them and referred to them as the "Jackass Cavalry." Poor planning and leadership resulted in Streight's 1,700-man force surrendering to Nathan Bedford Forrest, who had 500 men.[92]

Although dead mules were not as numerous or apparent as horse carcasses, some died from the same reasons as horses: overwork, lousy nutrition, disease, and enemy firepower. An excellent example of the overwork of horses and mules happened early in the war in 1861 in western Virginia, now West Virginia, pulling supplies over mountains' roads that were almost impassable because of mud that were several feet deep. Horses and mules could pull only half a load or less. A mule driver remembers watching a mule team run off a corduroy, sinking out of sight in mire and quicksand. The only part of the mules that were visible were the ear tips of the pole mule.[93]

Mules that ran off a corduroy road (John D. Billings, *Hardtack and Coffee*)

---

92 Billings, *Hardtack and Coffee*, 294.
93 Armistead, *Horses and Mules in the Civil War*, 123.

Another mule was more fortunate. Near Richmond, a mule with a heavy backpack was walking on the springers; the boards had been removed on a bridge high above the James River. The mule fell, tumbling in the air before hitting the water. Onlookers thought it was the end of the animal, but the mule came to the surface, swam to the shore, and shook himself with his backpack still intact, a testimony to the animal's toughness and skill of the backpacker.

HORSES

Unlike mules, which seem to have no attraction to humans, horses became fond of their owners. Despite this affection, they showed their disapproval. The riders' numerous injuries were the result of animals not wanting to do what the rider wanted. Charley, ridden by the bloodthirsty bushwhacker William Clarke Quantrill, had a mean temperament like his owner. Charley became a vicious animal; he would attack, bite, kick, and squeal when approached by others. Only Quantrill could control him. Near the end of the war, Charley was disabled when the main tendon in his right hind leg was cut when his shoes were being pared (trimming the roof).[94] Kangaroo was one of Grant's horses. It started as an ugly duckling but, with proper care, became a beautiful mount used by Grant during the Petersburg Campaign. It got its name from the habit of rearing on its hind feet and jumping forward when being mounted.[95] Captain Davis of the US Army had a horse that sat down on its haunches like a dog when the rider got off.[96]

---

94   Ibid. 62, 75.
95   Billings, *Hardtack and Coffee*, 829.
96   Hawkins, *Horses in Gray*, 62.

A horse that sat like a dog (John D. Billings, *Hardtack and Coffee*)

Stonewall Jackson's Fancy had the unique habit of lying down like a dog when resting. Jackson's widow, Anna, received Fancy after her husband's death. The widow referred to the horse as Old Fancy, who she vividly described as a rascal. He would use his mouth to lift latches and let down bars a man would use his hands for. He had a habit of letting himself out of his stable and letting all the other horses and mules out of theirs, leading them to the greenest pasture or grain field. Rail fencing was not a problem. Old Fancy used his mouth to lift off a number of rails so it was low enough to jump over.[97] Less friendly was George Meade's battle-scarred Baldy, known as "The Snapping Turtle" for his propensity to bite. Being wounded 14 times during the war probably did not help his disposition.[98] Union General George McClellan had a horse named Burns that had a unique habit. It had to be fed grain at a specific time each day. Despite where they were, the horse returned to the feeding area

---

97 Worman, *Civil War Animal Heroes*, 214-215.
98 Fairfax Downey, *Famous Horses of the Civil War*, (New York: Thomas Nelson & Sons, 1960), 25.

at a specific time, even during a battle. McClellan had to make sure to ride another mount during combat.[99]

Even President Lincoln was the victim of a runaway horse. General Benjamin Butler, in the spring of 1864, staged a review of his troops for Lincoln. He gave the president one of his two powerful mounts to ride: an impressive stallion named Ebony. The band's noise and artillery fire panicked Ebony, who suddenly ran full speed ahead. The president could not rein in the frightened horse. Lincoln's stove pipe hat fell off and was trampled by the hooves of pursuing horses. The president was in peril of injury or death. Finally, one of Butler's orderlies, riding a racehorse, overtook Ebony, rescuing the president.[100]

An officer under Jeb Stuart, William Blackford, had a horse, Comet, whose routine of warming himself on a cold morning entertained the cavalrymen and lessened camp boredom. On cold mornings, most horses huddle together to keep warm. But Comet had an exercise routine. He pawed one of his forefeet as fast as he could for as much as five minutes, then did the same for the rest. Once the cycle was completed, Comet kicked high in the air as onlookers applauded, and the horse concluded with a swish of his tail and loud snorts.[101]

THE CANTANKEROUS CAMEL

Shortly before the Civil War, Jefferson Davis, secretary of war under President Franklin Pierce, planned to form a camel corps to mount troopers in the hot, arid southwest on camels because they withstand dehydration much better than horses. And, they have an

---

99   Charles W. Russell, ed., *The Memoirs of Colonel John S. Mosby*, (Bloomington: Indiana University Press), 159.
100 Armistead, *Horses And Mules In the Civil War*, 129.
101 Hawkins, *Horses in Gray*, 172.

uncanny way of finding water. Camels can go eight to ten days without water, cover 30 to 40 miles daily, and get nourishment by eating prickly plants as they travel. Congress appropriated $30,000 to purchase camels. In 1856, 33 were imported from Africa and the Middle East; in 1857, 41 more were purchased. Camp Verde, Texas, became the home for both Bactrian (two humps) and Arabian (one hump) camels owned by the government. Commercial interests led to purchasing over four hundred camels brought to Texas, Alabama, and California, dwarfing that of the federal government. Camels were frequently used as draft animals by the military and civilians. After the Gold Rush and shortly before the Civil War, camel caravans were frequently seen between San Antonio and Los Angeles.[102] An attempt early in the Civil War to use camels to carry mail between US military posts in New Mexico Territory and California failed because commanders objected.

Davis' camel experiment never got a good foothold. This was partly because Davis' tenure as secretary of war ended, and the Civil War started with Davis as the president of the enemy. Confederates, in 1861, seized Camp Verde and about 80 camels and Union soldiers. The latter they made prisoners. The Union had control over camels in the southwest, but neither side seemed to know how to use camels. For a while, Confederates used camels to carry cotton. Others were just turned loose. When the war ended, the Union captured Camp Verde, sold the camels to the circus, gave them to zoos, or turned them loose in the desert. The last descendant of the army's camels seen in the desert was in 1941. In the United States today, there are approximately 3,000 camels owned mainly by private citizens.[103]

---

102 "History of Camels in the US," https://desertfarms.com.pages.history. "United States Camel Corps https://en.wipedia.org.wiki.United.States_Camel_. "The U.S . Army's Remarkable Camel Corps of the 1850's." https://:daily.istor.org.Archives_Most_Recent_Posts.
103 Hawkins, *Horses in Gray*, 173.

When the camels first arrived in the late 1850s, they could be challenging to manage. It took practice, and loads placed on them frequently ended up on the ground. Despite their superior strength and ability to tolerate a harsh, arid environment, their behavior could be offensive. A reporter for *The New Yorker* wrote, "…they were vicious, tended to cough up foul-smelling chunks of food, and made horrible groans that terrified the horse."[104] Camels have good memories and hold grudges. When mistreated, the offender was later the recipient of spitting, hissing, and biting. The malodorous smell of camels caused horses and mules to buck, rear up, or bolt. A Confederate handler of mules in 1862 contented camels were malingering and did indeed hold grudges.[105]

Robert E. Lee gave a more favorable view of camels while still in the US Army in the spring of 1860 as the temporary commander of the Department of Texas. Lee sent a reconnaissance to locate a campsite in a highly arid area in western Texas with a train of 20 camels and 25 mules. After five days, three mules had died, and nine mules had to be left because they could not continue. The camels endured the trip fine, causing Lee to praise the camels, "whose endurance, docility and sagacity" and "reliable service" prevented the reconnaissance failure.[106]

---

104   Ibid.
105   "United States Camel Corps," https://en.wipedia.org.wiki>United_States_Camel_C.
106   Rebecca Frankel, *War Dogs* (New York: St. Martin's Griffin, 2015), 78.

CHAPTER 6

THE BOND BETWEEN MAN AND BEAST

People are intrigued by animals. There is something about a different life form that stimulates the interest of most people. Two of the principal commanders of the Civil War, Lee and Grant, had a great appreciation of animals and the need to care for them. This applied not only to their mounts but also to other animals. Grant even questioned a mule driver about why he used such abusive language when giving orders to mules. Mistreatment of animals angered Grant. His temper reached an exceptional intensity when he saw a wagon team stuck in the mud. The swearing driver climbed from the wagon and brutally beat the faces of the horses with the butt end of his whip. The general shouted, "Stop beating those horses!" The driver, unaware it was the commanding general, continued beating a horse nearest the wagon and replied, "Well, who's driving this team, anyhow, you or me?" Grant replied, "I'll show you, infernal brute villain!" The driver was tied to a tree for six hours as punishment for his brutality.[107]

Lee's strong affection for Traveller caused him to oversee the treatment of his horse, including being present when Traveller was

---

107 Downey, *Famous Horses of the Civil War*, 102.

reshod. After the war, Traveller was allowed to graze in his front yard, and Lee affectionately touched the old war horse. Lee's fondness for animals extended beyond horses.[108] He had a pet cat and dog while away on military duty. After the war, one of Lee's favorite animals was a cow. Shortly before his death, Lee complained to his wife, "You do not mention the cow; she is of more interest to me than the cats and is equally destructive of rats."[109]

Canines are social creatures and were the dominant mascot and pet during the Civil War. Still, soldiers seemed to make pets out of whatever animals they came upon: four-legged, feathered, and reptiles, some of which seemed dangerous and unsuitable as pets. The dog and other pets were vital to the soldier's mental health. Although not critical for combat like horses and mules, they were morale boosters, providing an escape from the boredom of camp life, the horrors of warfare, and the reality of death or maiming in the next battle. Both sides used dogs in combat as soldier substitutes for advanced pickets. For example, during the Peninsular Campaign in 1862, Federals sent Newfoundlanders as advanced pickets ahead of their soldiers. The cavalry used dogs to clear the way before the horses, making dogs the primary target of Confederate fire that killed many of them.

The treatment of dogs in the Civil War was the most extreme of the animals associated with the war. It varied from fondness as a pet to extermination. Each side occasionally shot barking dogs that might reveal their location to the enemy. In his March to the Sea, Sherman wanted dogs eliminated, as did the state of Virginia. The war highlighted the problem of sheep-killing dogs, forcing several states, north and south, to consider regulations to increase control. By far, the most extreme was Virginia's proposal to kill all the dogs

---

[108] Worman, *Civil War Animal Heroes*, 150-151, 155.
[109] Ibid.

in the Old Dominion and use their carcasses to produce materials that would support the war. Others also considered dogs a nuisance. To solve this problem, dogs accompanying Union troops in boats on the Kanawha River on the way to Charleston, Virginia, in 1861, were thrown overboard. Many drowned, and a few were able to swim to the riverbank. Dogs were shot for fear of what they may do. An example was a large yellow dog shot in camp after he snapped at a soldier.

Dogs were numerous in the military and society. There were approximately one million canines in the southeast and thousands in the area of the Appomattox Courthouse at Lee's surrender, some taken back home by Union soldiers as souvenirs.

By contrast, dogs also had the closest relationship with soldiers than other war animals and were the brightest. Animals' intelligence is a controversial topic that is difficult to determine and is primarily based on their behavior. Historically, man has underestimated canine intelligence while others have overestimated it, given the dog's almost-human qualities. Psychologist Stanley Coren addressed the issue in his book *The Intelligence of Dogs: Canine Consciousness and Capabilities*. He points out that, like other animals and humans, intelligence varies. It varies among canines by breed and within breeds. Coren contends that dogs display three types of intelligence: adaptive, working, and instinctive. The degree of each may vary from dog to dog.[110]

THE BOND WITH EQUINES

The cavalry had fewer mascots and pets because their horses became the animals they bonded with the most. They shared life

---

110   Earl J. Hess, ed. *Animal Histories of the Civil War Era* (Baton Rouge: Louisianna State University Press, 2022), 14, 103, 174. Stanley Coren, *The Intelligence of Dogs* (New York: The Free Press, 1994), 126-127. Worman, *Civil War Animal Heroes*, 156.

and death experiences that cemented their bond. Confederate Lieutenant Colonel Blackford was an animal lover who had nine horses. One named Comet was speedy, as his name implied. He was a beautiful blood horse (good bloodlines) to which Blackford taught tricks. Unfortunately, Comet only served Blackford for a year; he was wounded in the neck in Fairfax County, Virginia, in late 1862 during a rainstorm.[111] A distraught and crying Blackford later recorded the event.

> ... blood spouted several feet in a stream as large as my finger ... [Comet] stood up. Turning his head and looking me full in the face with his large, beautiful eyes, as plainly beseeching assistance. I could not keep the tears from trickling down my cheeks, and from his eyes the tears of large drops fell in the agony he suffered as he gazed wistfully at me. I screwed my handkerchief into the wound and stopped the flow of blood; in a few moments, the nervous shock was passed, and I had hope of his recovery."[112]

Blackford had to leave the wounded Comet with a local farmer and came back days later during the night to get him. As Blackford led his cherished horse back from behind enemy lines, infection from the wounds erupted. Comet survived but was too injured to continue as a war horse.

Nathan Bedford Forrest's favorite mount was a dark chestnut, Roderick, who impressed men around him as an unusually loyal horse. He seemed fixated on Forrest and followed the cavalry leader around camp like a dog, even trying to enter Forrest's tent. Roderick's devotion to Forrest was moving during the horse's last battle. Roderick was wounded three times and struggled to move

---

[111] Hawkins, *Horses in Gray*, 137-138.
[112] William W. Blackford, *War Years with Jeb Stuart*, (New York: Charles Scribner's Sons, 1947), 136.

forward. Forrest took him to the rear and got a fresh mount. But Roderick got away and returned to the battlefield, jumping three fences on his way there. Just before reaching Forrest, he received his fourth fatal wound. He died with Forrest, his favorite person, by his side.[113]

With similar loyalty to her owner was John Hunt Morgan's striking black Thoroughbred mare, Black Bess. In 1862, while escaping from the enemy in Lebanon, Tennessee, Morgan and his men had to leave their horses, along with Black Bess, on one side of the Cumberland River as they crossed by a ferry boat that lacked room for their mounts. Looking back across the river, Morgan could see Black Bess galloping aimlessly, neighing pleadingly to find Morgan. The Federals captured her, and Black Bess became the property of a Union general.[114]

Black Hawk, a famous black stallion racehorse of Major General William B. Bate of the Confederacy, seemed to have perceptive powers or, at the very least, a strong bond with his rider. At the bloody Battle of Shiloh, Bate, known as "Fighting Billy," rode Black Hawk with a white saddle, which probably attracted enemy fire. A bullet shattered Bate's leg and went through Black Hawk. The wounded horse carried his injured rider to the rear, where Bate was taken inside a cabin. Black Hawk is said to have peered through the door, whinnied, sunk to the ground, and died. Bate, with a revolver in his hand, would not allow the surgeon to amputate his leg. He survived but had a limp.[115]

During Nathan Bedford Forrest's raid into North Carolina and Tennessee, he forded a river at Muscle Shoals. The river bottom was

---

[113] Ibid., 143.
[114] Worman, *Civil War Animal Heroes*, 199-200.
[115] Ibid., 268.

rocky and rough, and swift water dismounted men, one of whom was a young man named Powell. His horse floated downstream over a fall. The horse looked back up at Powell and started back up the river. All observers assumed the horse would go to the island on the other side of the river, which was an easier route. Instead, Powell's horse struggled and faltered, going upstream to reach Powell. Reaching Powell, the horse laid his head on his shoulder. They then joined their regiment on the island.

Confederate Alexander Hunter's horse, Maud, was unusually affectionate, and their bond was strong. Whenever Hunter camped on cool nights, he snuggled up against Maud, who squatted on her four feet and slept comfortably through the night. "In the morning," Hunter said, "she would never attempt to rise without licking my face, which would awaken me." She followed Hunter around like a dog. Maud also helped Hunter escape from the pursuing enemy by jumping a tall fence and through an almost impassable bog in North Carolina.[116]

CANINE COMPANIONS

The wag of the tail and consistent daily unrestrained enthusiasm and undivided attention of the canine to see their owner made the dog people's main animal companion. Regardless of your day, the dog is glad to see you, greeting you as if it were a reunion after years apart. Dogs, cats, and horses accept us the way we are; they are good listeners and companions. Touching the soft hair of a dog, the purring cat, or the silky coat of a horse is soothing, increases the bond, and psychologically benefits the human and animal.

---

[116] Alexander Hunter, *Johnny Reb and Billy Yank* (New York: Neale Publishing Company, 1905), 700-701. Worman, *Civil War Animal Heroes*, 17-19, 34, 36.

Dogs came to camps in several ways. They were brought from home by their owner, stolen from other companies, or just showed up. Numerous strays collected around camps for food. The number of dogs with a company at times became numerous. The 104th Ohio Infantry had so many dogs that it was known as the "barking dog regiment." Canines varied in size from Newfoundlands to large mastiffs, hounds, pointers, bulldogs, poodles, and mongrels. They also fought among themselves. Many would form a line to be fed. At times, they became so numerous that they were a nuisance. They indeed increased the noise level in the camp. They all barked when the drum corps played, others howled at bugle call, one barked at the colonel's voice, and all kept constantly barking during combat. Men taught their mascots tricks and found that dogs could find chickens and aid them in catching rabbits. During the Petersburg Campaign, a Union soldier sent a large Newfoundland dog to the Confederate lines carrying small items for sale, like coffee and newspapers. Confederates sent the canine back with tobacco for payment. The process was repeated.

At times, they became targets of enemy sharpshooters. A pack of dogs accompanied the 34th Massachusetts Infantry at the Battle of New Market in the spring of 1864. The regimental commander, Colonel William Lincoln, wrote when they charged, "Our dogs, of whom we had a small army, ran frolicking and barking before us, as they had done on drill. Receiving the fire of both lines, they were nearly all killed."[117] Attempts were sometimes made to protect mascots during combat. The Richmond Howitzers artillery did this for their little Jack Russell terrier mascot, Stonewall Jackson. This depended on their ability to catch him and drop him into an empty

---

117   Jacob Gantz, *Such Are the Trials*, (Iowa State University Press/Ames), 21.

compartment of a limber chest.[118] Other dogs were tied during a battle, but many just roamed about, unaware they were in harm's way of bullets. Their penchant to chase rolling cannonballs and shells, thinking it was fun, could kill them. A large white dog at Malvern Hill in 1862 was chasing a shell when it exploded, sending its shredded remains skyward.

George A. Custer in the spring of 1862 with what is believed to be a captured Confederate dog. (National Archives)

Jack and Sallie were two celebrity mascot dogs of the Civil War, described as bulldogs or bull terriers. Before the war, as a stray, Jack wandered into the Pittsburgh firehouse. Unwelcomed at first, his scrappiness and unfailing attendance on every fire call endeared him to the fire company, which bought him an expensive $75 silver collar.

---

118   George W. Adams, *Doctors in Blue*, (New York: Collier books, 1961), 115. Anne Palagruto, *Civil War Dogs and the Men Who Loved Them* (Middletown, Delaware: n. p., 2024), 16-17.

When the war began, the firefighters became members of the 102nd Pennsylvania Volunteers, and Jack became their mascot until 1864. He was with the men in the thick of battle, wounded several times and captured twice. The first time, he was imprisoned for six months and exchanged for a Confederate soldier. He escaped from his second capture and continued to be a vital part of the 102nd until he disappeared at Frederick, Maryland, in late December 1864, believed to have been killed for his valuable collar.

Jack (courtesy of Charles Harrell)

As a pup, Sallie was given to a captain in the 11th Pennsylvania Infantry Regiment and became its official mascot. Five pregnancies, raising pups, and being wounded in the neck did not deter her from being with her men during drill and combat, licking the hands of the injured and guarding the dead. Two months before the war ended, Sallie led her men into Petersburg, Virginia, in fierce fighting. Among the dead lay a medium-sized female bull terrier, shot in the head.[119]

The closest bond was between the dog and the owner or primary caretaker. This was evident even after the death of the owner. During the Battle of Gaines' Mill during the Peninsular Campaign in 1862, Confederate General Bryan Grimes saw a St. Bernard dog protecting the corpse of a Union colonel. During the final day at Gettysburg, a pet dog of a Confederate regiment, a mongrel named Grace, accompanied the Southerners in their attack at Culp's Hill. Union Brigadier General Thomas Kane noticed a limping dog riddled with bullets licking a soldier's hand and going between the lines, like he was looking for his dead master. The dog soon died. This was the enemy's dog, but Kane, in his official report, stated he was "struck by the animal's gallantry and loyalty to its human companions…as the only Christian-minded being on either side, I ordered her to be honorably buried." Grace was laid to rest with the dead of her 1st Maryland Infantry. Nearly half of its men were casualties during the three-day battle.[120]

---

119   Worman, *Civil War Animal Heroes*, 62-63.
120   Ibid., 80, 82.

A dog protects the body of his dead owner. (*Frank Leslie's Illustrated Newspaper*)

After the Battle of Fredericksburg in 1862, there was the moving scene of a dog laying in the Union camp on the northern bank of the Rappahannock River next to what his dead owner had left behind before the battle, waiting for his return. Lieutenant Louis Pfieff of the 3rd Illinois Infantry had his dog with him when he was killed during the bloody Battle of Shiloh. The dog stayed and licked his owner's wounds, and for a dozen days, the dog watched over his dead owner until his wife arrived to get her husband's remains. Similar canine devotion was shown at Shiloh by a young dog following Union Private John Ferguson from camp to camp. Two days after the battle, the faithful young dog was found lying on the chest of his lifeless owner. The sad scene of a dog lamenting the death of his owner was repeated throughout the war.[121] Dogs, cats, and horses with a strong bond with humans instinctively seem to sense when that person is ill, hurt, or dead.

---

121 Hess, *Animal Histories of the Civil War Era*, 14. Fred Lanting, "Dogs in the Civil War," thedogpress.com. Nicholas Picerno, "A Famous Dog of the Civil War," https://www.history net.com>-civil-war-dog-major. "Man's Best Friend Goes to War," https://www.gilderlehman.org>inline>PDF. Palagruto, *Civil War Dogs and the Men Who Loved Them*, 39.

AN ALMOST ENDLESS VARIETY OF MASCOTS AND PETS

Almost all animals soldiers came in contact with became mascots or pets. The most famous was a bald eagle named Old Abe, in honor of the Union president, who belonged to the 8th Wisconsin Infantry. Old Abe was captured as a young bird when an Indian cut down a tree with a nest and traded the young bird to another man. The new owner had trouble getting rid of the bird. Finally, he sold it to a militia company for $2.50. Legend has Old Abe flying over 36 battles during the Civil War. In reality, he went into battle fettered on a perch carried by a soldier marching along with the color guard. At the Battle of Corinth, the cord holding him was cut by an enemy bullet, and Old Abe flew a short distance over the battle line before being caught. Over the years, this became exaggerated. On another occasion, a bullet creased his feathers, leaving the eagle unhurt. In 1864, Old Abe was given to the state of Wisconsin, and it lived for 15 years in the basement of the state capitol. Old Abe lived for 44 years and died from smoke inhalation when a fire occurred in the capitol. After the war, Old Abe became a Union symbol and attended numerous Republican rallies, soldiers' reunions, monument dedications, and Fourth of July celebrations. He was a magnet for curious citizens.

Some critics complained about the cost of caring for Old Abe after the war. A Kansas newspaper went even further, calling the eagle's war record a hoax, claiming the eagle hid in a sutler's wagon and refused to come out during artillery and rifle fire. Around camp, he was a nuisance, a filthy and ugly creature that spread disease among the soldiers by eating buzzards.[122]

---

[122] Hess, *Animal Histories of the Civil War Era*, 216-222. Worman, *Civil War Animal Heroes*, 33-34. James A. Page, "The Story of Old Abe," famous Wisconsin war eagle on the 101st Airborne Division patch, https://www.army.mil>artile>the- strory of old abe. The Atlanta Cyclorama depicts Old Abe in its panoramic painting of the battle, but the eagle was not at the battle.

Old Abe (Library of Congress)

Lesser known were eagles used as mascots in other regiments. Some mascots were dangerous and led to human injury. Several regiments had the fierce badger and wildcat as mascots. A pelican was the mascot of a Louisiana unit. One unlikely mascot was the unimpressive buzzard brought into one camp. An Illinois cavalryman had a chameleon kept in a bottle as a pet. Another soldier had several baby mice he cared for in his pocket. A crow was a mascot in another camp. The Confederate ship *Sultana* had an alligator mascot that perished when the ship exploded. Another boat had an alligator that bit a sailor when he tried to get the alligator out of his bed. The reptile was put ashore. Several ships had bears; one on the USS *Wabash* bit the quartermaster so badly, his leg was amputated. The bear was put on shore the following day. Cats were popular aboard ships and in camps to control mice and rats. Blacksnakes, raccoons, foxes, and dogs were also brought aboard ships for entertainment. Pigs, chickens, geese, and lambs were kept on ships for food. In camps, chickens were usually eaten, and a few generals kept them for their eggs. The most famous chickens were those that were skillful cock fighters. The brutal activity of cock fighting was very popular with the troops, who bet heavily on the outcome. Success in cockfights kept a rooster out of the frying pan.[123]

One famous mascot was a dromedary camel: Old Douglas of the 43rd Missouri Infantry. Although he scared the horses, Old Douglas was docile and well-liked by the men. He was killed during the Vicksburg Campaign by a Confederate sharpshooter, and his bones were later found and made into rings and other ornaments and sold. Legend has Old Douglas eaten by starving Confederates, but the corpse could not be reached because of the danger of enemy fire. A memorial marker honoring him was installed in a Vicksburg cemetery in 2006.[124]

---

[123] Workman, *Civil War Animal Heroes*, 12-15, 85-90, 107-110, 118-119, 137-140.
[124] Hawkins, *Horses in Gray*, 176-178. Workman, *Civil War Animal Heroes*, 94-103.

CHAPTER 7

THE TORMENTORS

War was brutal on both men and animals. Added to their suffering were the incessant bites of insects that continually tormented them, causing discomfort and illness. For men, lice were the paramount tormentor, followed by the fly. Many other parasites plagued man and beast. The human body was the favorite habitat for mosquitos, chiggers, mites, bed bugs, gnats, scabies, and intestinal worms. During combat, coming in contact with bees could be painful. Seeing or stepping on poisonous snakes unnerved soldiers and was life-threatening. Although they were nocturnal, coming in contact with a skunk could lead to being sprayed with their sickening, enduring, and overpowering malodorous secretion. For the Civil War prisoners, large, vicious guard dogs were tormentors. Military camps were breeding grounds for lice, fleas, flies, and mosquitoes. Latrines were improperly located and should have been covered with fresh dirt daily but were left uncovered. Men relieved themselves anywhere on the campground, requiring vigilance where one walked. Garbage was also scattered about. The lack of human hygiene created a favorable environment for parasites. Many soldiers rarely changed their clothes or bathed.

An Iowa soldier noted, "I have seen men literally wear out their underclothes without a change, and when they threw them off they would swarm with vermin like a live ant hill when disturbed."[125] One soldier searched in vain for his lost socks. He found he was wearing his socks when he bathed and washed away the layer of dirt from his feet. Prison filth provided an ideal environment for bed bugs, flies, lice, mites, and fleas that continually tormented the bodies of the malnourished and debilitated prisoners. Flies not only harassed prisoners but laid eggs on bandaged wounds that hatched into maggots. Chiggers were another annoying mite that penetrated the skin, creating unending itching that Mother Bickerdyke, a famous Civil War nurse, said could only be solved by rubbing the irritated site with bacon rind.

INSECT TORMENTORS

Lice, which soldiers called graybacks, were unwanted and relentless companions in Civil War military life. John D. Billings accurately recorded in his classic *Hardtack and Coffee*, "Like death, it [louse] was no respecter of persons . . . It inserted its bill as confidingly into the body of the major-general as of the lowest private."[126] Men were embarrassed and felt guilty or disgusted about having lice and attempted to be secretive in their futile attempts to get rid of them. Others did not seem to care. Some never bathed during the entire years of their military service. A much-used and unsuccessful way was to pick graybacks off one's body and clothing. It was time consuming and futile picking them off clothing, even for the man who picked 52 from a shirt. Men would take themselves to secluded places and sit with their garments for the "knitting" work, examining

---

[125] James I. Robertson Jr., *Soldiers Blue and Gray* (Columbia, South Carolina: University South Carolina, 1988), 152-153, 200-201.
[126] Billings, *Hardtack and Coffee*, 81-83. Earl J. Hess, ed., *Animal Histories of the Civil War Era* (Baton Rouge: Louisiana University Press, 2022), 135-145.

every fiber with great intensity, looking for graybacks. An Alabamian soldier told his wife and children, who wanted to visit him at camp, to stay away because "If you were here the Boddy lice would eat up the children in one knight in spite of all we could do; you dont hav any idea what sort of animal they are."[127]

Looking for graybacks (John D. Billings, *Hardtack and Coffee*)

During warm weather, some soldiers tried to wash away lice by placing their clothes in a nearby stream at night with a rock on them to prevent them from being washed away. Equally unsuccessful was holding infested clothing over a fire. The only method that worked was boiling infested clothing in a large pot, like a mess kettle.[128]

---

127   Bell Irvin Wiley, *The Life of Johnny Reb* (New York: Bobbs-Meier publishers, 1943), 251.
128   Ibid.

Boiling clothes to get rid of graybacks (John D. Billings, *Hardtack and Coffee*)

Soldiers amused themselves with lice races involving bets on which louse was the fastest. They would use their tin plates as a racetrack. The first around the dinner plate was the winner.[129]

Fleas were another great tormentor of human and animal bodies. Ticks gorged themselves, causing itching and swelling to mini balloons. No amount of movement of the tail or flinching of the skin by a horse, mule, or steer prevented or significantly lessened the incessant blood-sucking bites of horseflies and smaller varieties that swarmed over their backs, stomachs, and faces. One soldier considered fleas a greater menace than graybacks and wrote, "We could smoke away gnats, smash a mosquito, and scald the Graybacks, but the ubiquitous flea---he was too much for us." Another warrior believed there was no use killing them because fleas

---

[129] Peter J. Parish, *The American Civil War* (New York: Holmes & Meier Publishers, 1975), 146.

were too numerous.[130] They were the worst in Civil War prisons. At Andersonville, flies crawled over the faces and into the mouths of the sleeping sick, laying eggs in wounds and sores. Their bodies were so covered with mosquito bites, they appeared to be suffering from measles. Fleas were not only a problem for men but found dogs and cats equally desirable targets.[131]

Parasites did not just inflict annoying pain but impaired the health of men and animals. Ticks, fleas, mites, lice, and mosquitoes exposed men to typhus, reoccurring fevers, malaria, and amoebic dysentery, the most lethal of diarrheal infections that affects not only intestines but other organs, including the brain and lungs. Parasites impacted the war. The malaria outbreak that plagued the Union Army in the summer of 1863 slowed its effectiveness, and the outbreak of malaria among Confederates was a factor in the success of the Union in capturing Vicksburg.

Parasites also imperiled the health of animals. Flies transmitted diseases. The small gnat can kill large livestock and chickens by getting in their airways, causing anaphylactic shock. Gnat bites can also result in a gnat larva entering the skin, becoming a parasite that lives in a ligament in the horse's neck, known as onchocerciasis, causing extreme itching in the neck and belly.[132]

Flies transmitted many diseases to horses, cattle, and deer, such as anthrax, anemia, and anaplasmosis; the latter had a 50 percent mortality rate among southern cattle. An Illinois colonel wrote he had never seen house flies so thick. Two Union officers had their horses stung to death by flies, which attacked the genitalia.[133]

---

130   Futch, *History of Andersonville Prison*, 37, 45.
131   Ibid.
132   Karen Griffiths, "HORSEPLAY: Gnats can cause horses health problems," https://www.peninsuladailynews.com>life>horsepia.
133   Steiner, *Disease in the Civil War*, 175.

Internal parasites, like roundworms and tapeworms, debilitated the health of humans and animals. The number of soldiers who had worms in the Army of the Potomac in 1862 was 515, a small number compared to other disorders suffered by soldiers but still a significant health hazard.[134]

REPTILES

Snakes, bees, and non-reptiles like skunks did not seek out humans and animals but responded to the disruption of their environment. They were only occasional annoyers compared to continual parasitic annoyance. Reptiles were abundant on many battle sites, especially in the mountains, soldiers faced throughout the war. At Cheat Mountain in Virginia (now West Virginia) in 1861, combatants faced numerous rattlesnakes, copperheads, black snakes, and an endless variety of snakes everywhere. Soldiers died from poisonous snake bites, but amazingly, the number was not significant. *The Medical and Surgical History of the Rebellion* does not mention deaths from snake bites.[135] A Michigan infantryman wrote to his family in the summer of 1863, "The alligators eat some soldiers, but if the soldiers would stay out of the river, they would not be eaten." There appears to be no other attacks by large animals like bears, wolves, or mountain lions. If soldiers were killed by these animals, it would probably have been when they were isolated from their main force.

Snakes caused emotional trauma for soldiers. Such was the experience of Confederate Major-General Patrick Cleburne when he woke up with a rattlesnake curled up with him in his blanket. He was fortunate to escape without being bitten. Soldiers became highly excited when large water moccasins started dropping on the deck of their ship from willow trees that lined the bayous. A soldier in western Virginia

---
134   Barnes, *The Medical and Surgical History of the War of the Rebellion*, 30.
135   Ibid. 30-32.

RELUCTANT PARTICIPANTS

(now West Virginia) wading a stream to return to his Union camp at Elkwater shot another soldier. Frightened by a snake in the water near him, the soldier fired at the reptile but instead hit a comrade.

Snakes were also a danger to civilians, especially those living in caves in Vicksburg. Not only were their lives in peril from the ceaseless Union artillery fire but also the abundance of serpents. One cave dweller, Margaret Lord, wrote, "We were . . . in hourly dread of snakes. The vines and thickets were full of them, and a large rattlesnake was found one morning under a mattress on which some of us had slept all night."[136]

There were several remedies for snake bites in the mid-1800s. One involved putting gunpowder on the bite and igniting the powder, thinking it would burn the venom out. Ammonia was a popular remedy in the 1700s and 1800s, with many carrying small bottles of it to pour on snake bites. A painful and common remedy was to cut out as much of the wound as possible and, hopefully, the poison. Another belief was that drinking a lot of whiskey would counteract the snake venom when, in reality, it speeds up the absorption of snake venom.

Another camper, Mrs. Jones, the wife of a Confederate general, was forced to sleep in a tent on a bluff overlooking the Mississippi River during the Siege of Vicksburg. She recalled, "Lizards were very abundant. The feet of our cots were put in jars of water . . . to keep them off our beds. We could hear their little feet scratching as they raced after each other over the tents."[137]

---

[136] Wheeler, *The Siege of Vicksburg*, 209.
[137] "Snake Bite Remedies of the 1800s," https://cdsn5-ss2.sharpschool.com/UserFiles?....Richard Wheeler, *The Siege of Vicksburg* (New York: Thomas Y. Crowell, 1978), 185, 209.

BEES

Bees attacked with stinging fury when their habitat was interrupted. Recipients of their fury were Union soldiers from Pennsylvania during the Battle of Antietam when a Confederate shell hit beehives in a farmer's orchard, putting the Union men in harm's way with bee stings and life-taking enemy bullets. The stings made the soldiers run, jump, duck, and roll in the grass. Fearing the panic would spread, the men were ordered to double-quick to outdistance the bees.[138] On other occasions, soldiers were stung by yellow jackets, wasps, hornets, and bumblebees.

During John Mosby's attack on a Union supply train at Berryville, Virginia, in 1864, his men had the misfortune of unlimbering an artillery piece over a yellow jacket's nest, forcing one man to endure their stings as he pulled the artillery to safer ground.[139]

One of the most moving situations involving bees was during the start of the Second Battle of Bull Run at Brawner's Farm. A boy, 15, and his father were among the Confederates responding to an attack by the Union on Stonewall Jackson's forces. At the end of the battle at Brawner's Farm, the father came upon his son calling out in the darkness. "Hello, Charley, my boy, is that you?" In a shrill voice, the boy responded. "Oh, yes. Father, my leg is broken but I don't want you to think that is why I am crying for; I fell in a yellow-jacket's nest and they have been stinging me ever since. That is what makes me cry, please pull me out."

After enduring such unimaginable pain from the bee stings and wound, the lad soon died in his father's arms.

---

138 James V. Murfin, *The Gleam of Bayonets* (New York: Thomas Yoseloff, 1966), 249.
139 John S. Mosby, *The Memoirs of Colonel John S. Mosby* (Bloomington, Indiana. *Indiana Press*, 1959), 291.

Despite being stung, soldiers wanted the sweetness of honey and, when not in combat, foraged for it by carrying off beehives. To counter the thief of their bees, Confederate women tied the hives together, making them more difficult to steal. Beeswax was also valued to make a salve that soothed sore feet.[140]

PRISON DOGS

The Confederates used a few dogs to guard Civil War prisoners, but not the Union. Any animal in a Civil War prison was in great peril of being eaten by the prisoners. The exceptions were a giant dog, a Russian bloodhound and a bulldog mix named Hero, used as a guard dog at Libby and Castle Thunder prisons in Richmond, Virginia, and the dogs at Andersonville Prison in Georgia. They have been depicted as both vicious and harmless. Hero was solid black, seven feet long, three feet eight inches tall, and weighed 180 pounds. He had been trained to fight bears and was quite proficient. His owner claimed Hero fought three grown bears and was the victor. His formidable appearance kept prisoners in line, but he was amicable and played with them. According to Rev. J. L. Burrows, who wrote *Recollections of Libby Prison,* there was absolutely nothing formidable about the dog but his size. He was one of the best-natured hounds whose head I ever petted and one of the most cowardly." He would run from smaller dogs, and "I never heard that he bit anything but the bones that were thrown to him." Another inmate said Hero was Friendly, but you did not want to make him mad.

---

140   Hess, *Animal Histories of the Civil War Era*, 126.

Hero (Library of Congress)

Conditions at Civil War prisons inspired escape attempts. The stockade prison at Andersonville was the most egregious of all prisons. All inmates suffered from disease, illness, starvation, and maltreatment that took the lives of a third of the Andersonville Prison population. Captain Henry Wirz was in charge of the infamous Confederate prisoner-of-war camp. He used dogs to prevent the escape of prisoners and catch those attempting to escape. Dogs were not always successful in capturing escapees. Prisoners who were unsuccessful in escaping were not fed, and their food was given to the dogs that helped catch them. The traditional view contends dogs attacked and maimed Union prisoners who attempted to escape. Wirz referred to these dogs as the:

> Hounds of Hell, apparently intending them to kill or injure prisoners who attempted to escape. During the trial of Wirz that preceded his execution for the conditions at Andersonville Prison, testimony was given that a prisoner who attempted to escape was 'overtaken by hounds and a portion of his ear was torn off and his face mangled.'[141]

Robert S. Davis, in his book *Andersonville Civil War Prison*, gives a different view: "Contrary to accounts of personal memories, no first-hand account has been found of these mongrels attacking anyone." Trained to find but not harm escaped slaves, the dogs played with the prisoners they tracked down while waiting [for the guards' arrival]."[142]

The dogs were owned by Confederate Private Edward Turner and trained to hunt opossums, raccoons, and runaway slaves. When pursuing escapees, Turner divided them into packs of five dogs with a lead dog that was part bloodhound. Dog packs and mounted guards circled the stockade to prevent prisoners from escaping during the night.[143]

---

[141] Robert Scott Davis, *Andersonville Civil War Prison*, (Charleston, South Carolina: History Press, 2010), 30-32.
[142] Ibid.
[143] Ibid., 30-32.

Andersonville Prison (Library of Congress)

RATS

Phoebe Pember, the matron at Chimborazo Hospital in Richmond, describes how rodents annoyed patients, especially at night. Rats ate all the poultices from patients during the night, and others dragged away pads filled with bran placed under wounded limbs. One rat is claimed to have eaten the infection of a soldier with a wounded foot that was so bad, surgeons refused to operate, fearing lockjaw. The rodent's surgery cleared the infection and enabled the patient to recover.[144]

---

144   Marilyn Seguin, *Dogs of War* (Boston: Branden Books, 1998), 59.

DISRUPTORS OF THE DEAD

In the aftermath of battles, dead, wounded, and insects created ungodly sights on the battlefield. Flies swarmed over swollen and darkened bodies, which rapidly deteriorated. Corpses covered with maggots that feasted upon the remains' eyes, nose, mouth, and other body parts. Shallow graves made it easy for chickens scratching for food to expose human remains. The most common farm animals that disturbed the dead were unpenned hogs in the South. They ate the human corpses and could be seen running about with a foot or other human body part in their mouth. Crows picked the eyes out of the dead on battlefields.

Humans also played a role as disrupters of the dead. After the Battle of Ball's Bluff in 1861, as Union prisoners were being marched through the First Bull Run battlefield to the railroad in Manassas to be shipped south, a Confederate took a board and dug up a Union body, taunting the Yankee prisoners. Union and Confederates buried their own dead with more care. The enemy dead were out in shallow graves or tossed into gullies; the dirt covering them often soon washed away, exposing arms and legs that could be seen sticking out of the ground. After the First Battle of Bull Run fought on July 21, 1861, Confederate spent the winter in nearby Centreville and clashed with Union forces as they both were foraging for hay in the area of Dranesville, Virginia, about 20 miles away.

During the winter of 1861-1862, to break the boredom, Confederates camped at Centreville made numerous visits to the Manassas Battlefield. They were especially drawn to the burial sites of the bright-colored uniforms of the New York Zouaves. Confederates used fence rails to pry up bodies to get buttons off their clothes. One Confederate sent his wife samples of hair from a Zouaves head and a tooth from an artillery horse. In December 1861, they dug up a

Federal artilleryman's body and were amazed to find that from the waist down, the flesh was firm and well-preserved. Finding this difficult to believe, all who passed by took a rail and turned the body to get a complete look. After the war, farmers in Gettysburg and elsewhere had to restrict their plowing because they were plowing up bodies. At many battle sites, there were numerous horse bones. Some proposed they be ground up and used as fertilizer, but opposition prevented this from happening. Opponents argued that making fertilizer from their bones was disrespectful because the horse had served honorably and deserved respect.[145]

---

145   Poland, *The Glories of War*, 540-541.

CHAPTER 8

HUNGER TRUMPS AFFECTION

The nourishing of men and animals was vital to their existence and performance in the military. The threat of eating pets, mascots, horses, mules, and rats was unlikely when food was abundant. But when driven by hunger and starvation from the lack of traditional fare, they became top menu items out of necessity, as did the intensity of foraging.

BEEF: A VITAL PART OF THE MILITARY DIET

Cattle were an invaluable source of food for the military. United States Army regulations in 1861 stated the daily rations for Union soldiers should be one pound, four ounces of fresh or salt beef or 12 ounces of pork or bacon. These were supplemented with other foods. Men wanted more vegetables but would go for weeks without them, leading to cases of scurvy. The official rations for Confederates were supposed to be similar to those of the Union, with less beef. Providing beef and other food items for more than a million men in the Union Army and nearly a million in the Confederate forces was difficult for commissaries to fulfill. The Union commissaries successfully fed their army by purchasing over three million cattle during the four-year war. After the first year of the war, Confederate commissaries would fall short, obtaining only a fraction of what the Federal government had purchased. To solve this problem, in 1862, the Confederate Commissary Bureau awarded contracts to civilian agents to find and bring in beef.[146] This would ultimately fail to provide enough beef. As the war continued, beef became more challenging to get, especially in the South. Soldiers on both sides turned to foraging, taking from farms, and, in extreme situations, eating what they did not normally consume. With the shortage of beef, the South ate more pork. Unlike in the North, hogs were not penned in and roamed over the region, making them foraging targets. It is estimated that nearly seven million hogs were killed during the Civil War, ten animals for each human fatality. When Kentucky, Maryland, and Missouri stayed in the Union, Confederates lost access to one-third of the South's hogs. Unlike the Union, Confederate commissaries did not have access to meat packing centers like those in Cincinnati and Chicago; they had the expensive task of paying for the rounding up of hogs from the interior and driving hundreds of hogs to Confederate camps. Southerners preferred pork to beef.[147]

Starving Confederates in 1864 were living off a one-third pound of bacon a day at Petersburg. One Confederate was able to catch a muskrat and skin and dress his catch. Then, for some strange reason, he buried it for a day or two, dug it up, and eagerly ate it. Another Confederate, leaving from a visit to a Petersburg widow, grabbed her gray cat in the yard and served it as a rabbit with garlic the next day to his mess. They were all aware it was a cat. Indicating the dire situation, Lee stated in August 1864, corn to feed the Southern soldiers was exhausted.

---

146 Edward Boykin, *Beefsteak Raid*, (New York: Funk & Wagnalls, 1960), 44.
147 Hess, *Animal Histories of the Civil War Era*, 139-140.

Much better off was Captain Elisha Hunt Rhodes of the 2nd Rhode Island Volunteers, who made a pet of a young sheep he named Dick from a flock brought to his camp from foraging in Clifton, Virginia. Dick, despite a belligerent disposition, became the mascot of the company and was taught tricks by the men and followed Rhodes everywhere he went on foot and horseback. Dick impressed and amused many when he joined officers during a dress parade and marched with them. Dick accompanied Rhodes and his men when they moved from Middletown, Virginia, to Washington. There, Dick's fate dimmed due to the lack of cash. Rhodes recounts, "[we] sacrificed our sentiment and sold poor Dick to a butcher for $5.00 and invested the proceeds of the sale in bread and Bologna sausage."[148] This raises the question of how strong Rhodes and his men's attachment to this sheep was. To Rhodes and the men, Dick was food and, secondarily, a pet.

The attitude toward animals and nature determined their treatment by humans. Were animals in existence solely for man's exploitation, or were they a vital part of the environment which needed to be conserved? Indeed, those who saw animals as sentient beings with emotions and feelings made many question the traditional treatment of animals and led to animal rights organizations. However, for the Civil War soldier, the view of animals was primarily as food. Many at war and in civilian life never thought about the rights of animals and followed traditions of hunting and viewing animals as food. According to Kelby Ouchley, who researched the attitudes of several hundred Union and Confederate soldiers, only 43 percent of Union and 26 percent of Confederates showed some degree of appreciation for animals other than food. One was George Dallas Mosgrove who, despite the need for food, decried the slaughter of rabbits in east Tennessee during the winter of 1863-1864 by Confederates, calling

---

[148] Seguin, *Dogs of War*, 54-55.

it "the greatest wholesale slaughter I ever witnessed" in war. Two to three thousand men surrounded a hundred-acre open field. When the mass of men accompanied by beating drums reached the center of the field, Mosgrove described it as "a pitiful and a ludicrous sight to see the countless little animals, timid and frightened, vainly trying to escape. After the slaughter ended, officers carefully divided the mounds of dead rabbits between all companies."

Combat was traumatic for other forms of wildlife. During the Battle of Chancellorsville in May 1863, when Jackson made a surprise attack on the Union, thousands of animals—birds, rabbits, squirrels, and quail—stricken with terror escaped the best they could through the air and on the ground. Wildlife during other battles had similar experiences.[149]

Most cattle were raised in the western states and were purchased from the North and South by commissaries and shipped to various armies that sent requisitions for the required rations. When stationary, cattle were placed in corrals. During the Petersburg Campaign in 1864, the Confederates found out the Union had 3,000 head of cattle near City Point that were lightly guarded in corrals 25 miles away. Confederate General Wade Hampton, with 3,000 men on September 14th, conducted a cattle raid that covered a hundred miles over a roundabout route that brought back to the Southern camp three days later 2,648 cattle; but, in the process, 50 men became casualties. Abraham Lincoln called the raid "the slickest piece of cattle stealing" he ever heard of. For days, Southerners taunted Union sentries, thanking them for the food and inviting them for dinner. However, the Beefsteak Raid, as it was called, did not solve the Confederate food shortage, providing only a short lull in their food insecurity. Fresh meat, if not properly preserved, will last only two

---

[149] Hess, *Animal Histories of the Civil War Era*, 102-103, 114-115.

days. If the beef from the raid could have been preserved, it would have fed 50,000 men for 40 days, but Confederates lacked the salt to preserve it and the feed to sustain the cattle.[150]

Beefsteak Raid (Library of Congress)

Up to 1863, Texas had three million cattle that fed the Confederacy. After Vicksburg, the Confederacy was split by the Union, who gained control of the Mississippi River, which blocked cattle from Texas and crossing the Mississippi River to the east. Unlike her other resources, the South had enough cattle to feed her troops but could not get them to the soldiers. In desperation, Confederates attempted to swim cattle across the Mississippi River only to have half the herd drown.

---

150   Boykin, *Beefsteak Raid*, 285-286.

The Confederacy in 1861

The Shrinking Confederacy at the end of 1863

The Civil War would give rise to the beef industry and the cattle kingdom. The wild cattle that roamed Texas grassland rapidly increased during the Civil War. By 1865, there were five million head of cattle. When the war ended, Texas and the South's economy were destroyed. A steer in Texas in 1865 was worth only $5.00 compared to $40.00 in Chicago and eastern cities. This led to the selling of cattle from Texas to eastern markets with a dense population. The problem was getting cattle to this market. The only way was to drive them from Texas to rail centers in Missouri and Kansas, known as the Long Drive (1866-1888). From Missouri and Kansas, cattle were shipped by rail to northern slaughterhouses and eastern markets. In the late 1880s, the Long Drive ended due to the shift to ranching after two frigid winters and dry summers that decimated the cattle.[151]

FLORIDA'S COW CAVALRY

Unable to access the vast number of cattle in Texas after July 1863, Confederates turned to Florida for beef. The state had under 400,000 cattle, far less than Texas, but it was a significant number to feed hungry Confederates. The animals were smaller due to the harsh and humid conditions they had to endure, but they could ward off diseases, especially those from the dreaded tick. Florida cattle weighed about 600 pounds and, once slaughtered, produced about 300 pounds of beef for consumption. The Confederate government divided Florida into five commissary districts in hopes of meeting the need for 3,000 cattle a week to feed her troops. Florida struggled to send 1,000 head of cattle each week, and it was not enough to feed her two armies, the Army of Northern Virginia and the Army of Tennessee. Pasture and fodder north of Florida declined, reducing the cattle size even more. The Federal cavalry attempted to stop

---

151 "1ˢᵗ Florida Special Cavalry Battalion," Wikipedia, . "Florida's "Cow Cavalry," https://www.3mergingcivilwar.com/cow.

the Confederates from sending cattle north of Florida. Raids by Confederate deserters further reduced the number of livestock, as did owners who were reluctant to sell cattle to the Confederate government that paid them with promissory notes.

In an attempt to protect Southern cattle sent northward, companies of cavalry were formed known as the "Cow Cavalry." It consisted of 900 men who were too old and boys who were too young to serve in the regular Confederate forces. These men and boys were also described as crackers. Supposedly, the term originated from the slave foreman cracking the whip when punishing slaves or someone using a whip dealing with draft animals. Northern writers expanded the meaning in the late 1800s to mean the hayseed faction of the South. Regardless of the social status of those in the Cow Cavalry, they drove cattle northward as fast as possible, which was vital in 1863 and 1864 to feed hungry Confederates. Still, ultimately, it was not enough to feed Southern forces.[152]

GETTING BEEF TO THE ARMIES

Most cattle were in the West, but New England contributed significantly to the Union. Cattle, by the hundreds of thousands for both sides, were sent by rail and ships to different armies and put in corrals. There, a regiment's commanding officer submitted a requisition to the commissary general certifying the number of rations of meat required. The appropriate number of cattle would then be sent to the armies and divided among the divisions.

Wherever the military forces went, the cattle followed behind them. Men were detailed as butchers and drovers and were excused from other military duties. Most of the slaughtering was done at night when they stopped moving. Steers were killed by being shot in

---

[152] "Beefsteak Raid," Wikipedia, https://en.wikipedia.org>wiki>Beefsteak_Raid.

the head where the curl of hair ends in the middle of the eyes. When moving, troops and trains used the roads, often forcing the cattle to travel elsewhere. Each herd had a lead steer used as a pack animal. He carried the equipment and cooking utensils of the drovers. He was docile and, during the day, followed the herdsman on horseback. If they were moving at night, the herdsman walked ahead, making a noise to settle the cattle. Drovers often had difficulty picking a way through underbrush, thorns, and brambles.

The lead steer (John D. Billings, *Hardtack and Coffee*)

Billings said, "It was a sad sight to see these animals, which followed the army so patiently, sacrificed one after another until but a half-dozen were left . . . It often took the butcher sometime before he could face one long enough to shoot."[153]

---

153   1st Florida Special Cavalry Battalion, Wikipedia, https://en.wikipedia.org/wiki/1st_ _Cavalry_ Battalion_ Florida. "Florida's Cow Cavalry," https://emergingcivil war.com/.../cow... "Embalmed Beef," https://www.encydlopedia.com.../embalmedbeef.

THE LAST STEER.

(John D. Billings, *Hardtack and Coffee*)

PREPARING BEEF FOR THE ARMY

The military faced two problems in providing beef for their soldiers. The first was getting it, and the second was preserving it. Both issues faced the Confederates and the Union. The Union had two rations: a marching ration of 16 ounces of hard bread (hardtack) and 12 ounces of salt pork or 20 ounces of fresh beef, sugar, and coffee. The above was reduced for camp rations. The Confederate menus were similar but smaller in quantity, with a shortage of coffee, and instead of hardtack, the bread was cornbread. The government menu was often unavailable, so soldiers' meals were often far different.

Beef for the soldiers was called "pickled beef" or "salt horse" and was prepared against decay for two years. It was so highly salted that it had to be soaked in water before eating, which removed the juices and salt and made it nearly inedible. Despite all the measures taken to preserve beef, it was often tainted, making soldiers sick because too much time had lapsed between slaughter and consumption.

Confederates lacked salt to preserve beef and were often forced to serve pork and bacon. The quality of pork issued by the Confederates and Union was worse than that of beef. Pork, called "sowbelly," was fat and rancid and described by one soldier ". . . as black as a shoe, on the inside, often yellow with putrefaction." Critics declared pork was indigestible. Many men wanted more vegetables, but they were spare, with soldiers going for weeks without them, which led to scurvy. Federal soldiers found meat canned by a Chicago packing company sent to them unappealing, calling the large surplus of canned beef that sat in depots when the war ended "embalmed beef."[154]

Billy Yank and Johnny Reb were also critical of the bread they were given. Hardtack, a flour and water biscuit, was so hard it was known as a "teeth duller" and had to be soaked or smashed to be eaten. One wag remarked that the B. C. on the cracker stood for its age, not the Boston Cracker Company. Even worse, hardtack was infested with maggots and weevils, justifying calling them "worm castles." Despite the unsavory infestation of insects, hungry soldiers ate the cracker with the vermin. To make hardtack more eatable, it was often fried with grease. In the enemy battle lines, Southerners damned unappealing cornbread that one soldier described as looking like a pile of cow dung that baked all day in the sun. Dissatisfied with the ration given to them, soldiers looked elsewhere. A few supplemented their diet by purchasing unhealthy sweets from sutlers, but most could not afford the high prices.[155] Hunting and foraging were more successful as soldiers took from local farmers, reducing their livestock and grain and burning fence rails for cooking.

---

[154] Billings, *Hardtack and Coffee*, 114-117.
[155] Ibid.

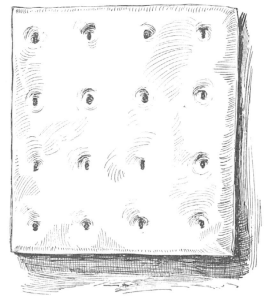

A HARD-TACK — FULL SIZE.

(John D. Billings, *Hardtack and Coffee*)

FRYING HARDTACK.

(John D. Billings, *Hardtack and Coffee*)

RELUCTANT PARTICIPANTS

As bad as the food was, inexperienced cooks made it worse. Cooking was first done in individual squads, each taking turns cooking. This shifted to inexperienced cooks for companies, despite the United States Sanitary Commission lobbying unsuccessfully to get a professional cook for each company and, in 1863, requiring company cooks to be trained.[156]

A Union Army Cook.

(Library of Congress)

DESPERATION DIETS

When traditional food was unavailable, hunger drove men to eat what was normally unacceptable, like dogs, horses, cats, mules, rats, and shoe leather. Even dogs considered pets around camps were victims. But the greatest threat to dogs was in Confederate and

---

156   George W. Adams, *Doctors in Blue*, (New York: Collier Books, 1961), 178-185. Hess, *Animal Histories of the Civil War Era*, 156.

Union prisons. If dogs were not protected, they were snatched and became meals.

Eating horses and mules, known as hippophagy, was practiced in ancient times and a few select areas later. By the Civil War, there was an aversion to horse and mule meat. Even as early as 1861, mules were eaten, according to a soldier from Connecticut who wrote home, claiming the commissary had issued "so much mule meat that the ears of the men had grown three and half inches." Servers sometimes claimed they were serving beef to avoid offending those who opposed hippophagy.[157]

During the Siege of Vicksburg, hunger drove people to eat horses, mules, and rats. A resident of the besieged city recorded in her diary, "Rats are hanging dressed in the market for sale with mule meat; there is nothing else." The price for a rat was $2.59. The president of the Confederacy, Jefferson Davis, is rumored to have endorsed the eating of rats and served them in the Confederate White House.

Eating rats was a common practice in Civil War prisons. Rats were so popular as food among the men in the Union prisoner-of-war camp at Rock Island (an island between Iowa and Illinois), they became scarce. At Camp Douglas in Chicago, called "The North's Andersonville," a dog of one of the prison officers wandered into camp and became a meal. In defiance, the prisoners posted on the bulletin board, "For want of meat. The dog was eat." Southern prisoners at Rock Island had eaten four dogs in ten months. One was the camp sutler's pet dog. At Camp Chase in Columbus, Ohio, prisoners caught a cat, soaked it in salt water overnight, and added onions, making it a stew. When Camp Douglas was expanded, half-starved

---

[157] Armistead, *Horses and Mules in the Civil War*, 82.

prisoners, according to one prisoner, captured and ate thousands of rats. No animal was safe in a Civil War prison.

When prisoners were served food, it was far from adequate and nourishing. J. Osborn Coburn kept a diary of his experiences as a prisoner in the shelterless camp on Belle Isle in Richmond. They often were served a bean soup that was "very wormy and musty." Water was taken from the James River and boiled for several hours. Each prisoner received about a quart of bean soup with a few beans, and it was clear enough that you could count the sparse number at the bottom of your serving. Another prisoner analyzed the "soup as 20 percent maggots, 30 percent beans, and 50 percent water." The cornbread served with the soup was brought to the prison in "vermin-infested blankets."

Civil War prisoners driven by extreme hunger would eat whatever they could get their hands on—things that often offend and shock people today. At Point Lookout, a prisoner-of-war camp in Maryland, an inmate found a dead seagull that had washed up on the beach. He ate the bird even though the bird had been dead for over a month. At all prisoner-of-war camps, men searched the grounds for old bones or scraps of food and plugs of tobacco previously chewed by someone else. At Camp Douglas, men gathered around an open sewer, grabbing scraps of food that flowed from the hospital, eating it like hungry animals. Another prisoner threw up his supper on his blanket. The following day, he threw out several pieces of meat that remained on the blanket. Another prisoner came along, picked them up, and ate them.[158]

So extreme was malnutrition in prison camps that men became too weak to walk, grew sick, and died. At Belle Isle, men died at the

---

[158] J. Osborn Coburn, *Hell on Belle Isle* (Bryan, Ohio: Faded Banner Publications, 1997), 128-129. Roger Pickenpaugh, *Captives in Gray*, (Tuscaloosa: University of Alabama Press, 2009), 194-195.

rate of eight to ten a day. Bodies were stacked up in a pile in the camp for over a week before burial, presenting a depressing sight for overcrowded prisoners housed only in tents, constantly suffering from lack of food, clothes, shelter, medical care, and filth. Photographs reveal men who were living skeletons void of flesh and muscle, as if they were only bones covered with skin.

CHAPTER 9

ANIMALS AS MILITARY TARGETS

Animals were military targets for seizure throughout the war and the target of guns during combat, but as the war went on, animals became a much larger target. They became part of the Union's strategy to destroy the South's agricultural, industrial, and rail systems and the will of Southerners to continue fighting. Expanding the attack on the South beyond the battlefield has been referred to as total war. The seizure and destruction of livestock and crops of the enemy became a significant element in the Union's strategy to eliminate the agricultural resources of the Confederacy and impede its ability to feed the Confederate Army. An additional objective included getting rid of annoying guerrillas like John Mosby. Two prominent examples of the Union's attempt to carry out this strategy in 1864 are Sheridan's burning of the Shenandoah Valley and Sherman's destruction of Georgia in his March to the Sea and into the Carolinas. Both targeted areas were vital in feeding Confederates. The Union's expanding strategy became even more ominous for the Confederacy because of her previous diminished resources due to the loss of territory to the Union, which shrunk the Confederacy. The Union forces in 1863 controlled the Mississippi River, splitting

THE BURNING OF THE SHENANDOAH VALLEY

After Jubal's attack on Washington during the summer of 1864, victory over Union forces in the Second Battle of Kernstown, and the capture and burning of Chambersburg, Pennsylvania, General Grant sent General Philip Sheridan to the Shenandoah Valley with instructions to "whip" Jubal Early. Sheridan did just that during the fall of 1864 at the battles of Winchester, Fisher's Hill, and Cedar Creek. The Union negated Confederates using the Great Valley as an invasion corridor to the north, but it remained the vital breadbasket for feeding Lee's army, despite a 50 percent reduction in grain production due to the labor shortage and fighting during the 1862 Valley Campaign.[159]

To help win the war, Grant wanted to destroy the Confederate breadbasket for feeding Lee's army, guerrilla activity, and the will of Southerners to continue fighting the war. To do this, Grant ordered Sheridan to devastate the Valley:

> Give the enemy no rest . . . Do all the damage to railroads and crops you can. Carry off stock of all descriptions and negroes, so as to prevent further planting. If the war is to last another year, we want the Valley to be a barren waste . . . so that crows flying over it . . . will have to carry their own provender with them . . . Leave nothing.[160]

---

159   Boatner, *The Civil War Dictionary*. 745. Ron Chernow, *Grant* (New York: Penguin Books, 2017), 445. John L. Heatwole, "The Burning: The Fire and Sword https://www.shenandoahwar.org.burning-article-2. Michael Mahon, *The Shenandoah Valley* (Mechanicsburg, Pennsylvania: Stackpole Books, 1999), 95-96.
160   "The Burning," https://www.aps.gov.the-burning-shenando.

The timing of Sheridan's burning of the Shenandoah Valley in the fall caused greater devastation than it would have during any other time of the year. Most of the farms' harvest was now near the farmhouse. The exception was corn in shock in the fields, which was easily burnable. Grains and hay were stored in barns, and hogs were ready to be slaughtered as soon as the weather was cold enough to prevent spoilage. Root cellars were full of vegetables. All farm products and animals were seized or destroyed. About one-third of the homes were burned, and virtually all the barns and their contents were taken or torched.

To carry out Grant's plan, Sheridan sent three divisions, each covering a section of the Valley and carrying out what is known as "The Burning," which many consider an example of total war. For days, starting on September 24th and terminating on October 8th, 1864, Union forces devastated the Great Valley from Staunton to Winchester, a distance of 70 miles and a width of 30 miles. Unlike the disorganized destruction by bummers under Sherman in the March to the Sea, destruction was carried out more systematically. But like the bummers, Sheridan's men had to take what they needed to eat from the farms. They generally ate exceptionally well, but food was sometimes in short supply, increasing pillaging. Homes were typically not to be burned, but any resistance made them fair game and increased the destruction and seizure of property. An example was the burning of 30 houses and outbuildings in Rockingham County as reprisal for the death of Sheridan's chief engineer, John Rodgers Meigs, at Dayton by three Confederate scouts.

Seeing their hogs slaughtered in their pens and livestock driven away or killed, their barns and houses burned, and farm implements destroyed shocked and traumatized residents and left them worried about how they could survive. For Valley residents, their world had come to an end. A number would leave. Among them was a civilian refugee train of 400 wagons that left Staunton to go north to survive. Some Union soldiers felt it was wrong to burn houses, leaving the women crying as smoke blotted out the sun. Other Federals thought they got what they deserved and pillaged the library and stole jewelry and other items.

One of the herds of confiscated livestock in the Valley was too large to control, so to thin the numbers, soldiers shot a large number. The corpses were put in piles with wood on top and turpentine poured on them. This and the burnings of homes and barns and the seizure of livestock and crops were outside the boundaries of what the South considered acceptable in warfare.

Sheridan had started his 13 days of devastation in the area of Staunton that was part of the upper Valley and moved northward to Winchester in the lower Valley. At the later part of the burning of the Shenandoah, Sheridan sent Major General Wesley Merritt with a force east of the Blue Ridge Mountains into Mosby's Confederacy in Loudoun and Fauquier counties to get rid of guerillas like John Mosby and "Lige" White and the guerillas in the Shenandoah Valley led by Harry Gilmer.[161]

For five days, from November 28th to December 2nd, 1864, the heart of Mosby's Confederacy was put to the torch—thousands of heads of livestock were driven from the area, and barns and mills were burned. No one was exempt, even Union supporters like the Quakers, who inhabited the northeastern part of Loudoun County. In 1873, federal law allowed loyal citizens to petition the government

---

161   John L. Heatwole, *The Burning* (Charlottesville, Virginia: Rockbridge Publishing, 1998), 187. Ray A. Neff, *Valley of the Shadow* (Terre Haute, Indiana: Rana Publications, 1987), 178-179. William G. Thomas III, "The Shenandoah Valley," https:///visitshenandoah.org. The terms upper and lower Shenandoah Valley are confusing. To go up the valley is to go south, and to go down the Valley is to go north.

to pay $61,821.13 for livestock losses. Another bill was repeatedly introduced for 30 years to pay Unions almost $200,000 for property losses, but the bill never passed.

A quick-thinking Quaker lady in Loudoun Valley thwarted Sheridan's men from torching her barn. The Union men on the burning expedition, "Burners," had the nerve to ask the woman for matches to burn her barn. Fearing retaliation if she failed to comply, she left them on the front porch and went to get the matches. Before she returned, she held the match heads in the steam from a tea kettle, which left them looking normal but prevented them from igniting when the soldier attempted to burn the barn.

A revealing account of the burning of Loudoun Valley was recorded by a Union soldier who participated in the incendiary action:

> The necessity of destruction is one of the many dark phases of war. Some idea of the destruction is shown by what was done by two regiments in one day: more than one hundred and fifty barns were burned, a thousand stacks of hay, and six flour mills, besides driving off fifty horses and three hundred head of cattle. It was the most unpleasant task we were ever compelled to undertake. It was heart-piercing to hear the shrieks of women and children and see even men crying and beating their breasts, supplicating for mercy on bended knee, begging that at least one cow—an only means of support—might be left. But no mercy was allowed. All that subsist guerrillas must be destroyed. If citizens would not themselves cease harboring guerrillas, then we must compel them to desist in the only way open to us. It was a terrible retribution on the county.

Despite the extensive destruction, it did not eliminate guerilla activity. Mosby continued to harass Union forces.[162] Similar scenes of pleading and panicking citizens occurred numerous times in the Shenandoah Valley.

Contrary to the view of the Union soldier about total war in Loudoun being repugnant but necessary, Southerners denounced it as straying beyond the acceptable to barbaric behavior in warfare. Confederate Henry Kyd Douglas ably articulated this in *I Rode with Stonewall*. He believed what Sheridan had done in the Shenandoah Valley and Loudoun Valley was undefendable, "for it was as an insult to Civilization and to God to pretend that the laws of war justify such warfare." Douglas was angry as he rode through the devastated Shenandoah Valley.

> I rode down the Valley [shortly after Sheridan's men had left] beneath great columns of smoke which almost shut out the sun by day, and in the night the red glare of bonfire, which, all across the Valley, poured out flames and sparks heavenward and crackled mockingly in the night air . . . I saw mothers and maidens tearing their hair and shrieking to Heaven in their fright and silent little children voiceless and tearless in their pitiable terror. I saw a beautiful girl, daughter of a clergyman, standing in the front door of her home while its stable and outbuildings were burning, tearing the yellow tresses from her head, taking up and repeating oaths of passing skirmishers and shrieking with laughter, for the horrors of the night had driven her mad.[163]

Sheridan reported that his forces, during the burn campaign, had destroyed over 435,000 bushels of wheat, 77,000 bushels of corn,

---

162   Poland, *From Frontier to Suburbia*, 213-214, 225. The Union officer supervising the operation estimated that 5,000 to 6,000 cattle, 4,000 sheep, and 6,000 hogs were driven off or destroyed.
163   Douglas, *I Rode with Stonewall*, 302.

20,000 bushels of oats, 20,000 tons of hay, 10,900 head of cattle, 12,000 sheep, 15,000 swine, 12,000 pounds of ham and bacon, 3,772 horses, 71 flour mills, and 12,000 barns. Sheridan seemed to exaggerate the amount of destruction. His figures are much larger than those of the reports of his subordinates who carried out the destruction. The reasons for this discrepancy are the rushed manner of the burning and the fact that only a small part of Sheridan's 6,000 men participated in carrying out the orders of destruction; some farms escaped ruin because the burning involved structures along the roads. According to Michael Mahon, author of *The Shenandoah Valley*, reports of Sheridan's officers show Sheridan's three cavalry divisions "actually spent little time savaging the countryside." But it had been enough. The residents in the Shenandoah Valley and Loudoun Valley were left destitute. "Nearly all the slaves, horses, cattle, hogs, and sheep" were gone. Their barns and houses had been robbed or burned. It was a challenge for residents to survive the winter.[164]

The surprising abundance of rabbits in Loudoun Valley allowed many residents to survive. Perseverance got them through. The lack of horses and equipment made it difficult to prepare for spring planting. One farmer had to use a horse and ox to plow his land. It must have been challenging getting the slow-moving ox to work successfully with the faster gait of the horse.

MARCH TO THE SEA

Sherman's March to the Sea from Atlanta to Savannah, Georgia, continued what Sheridan did in the Shenandoah Valley: destroy Confederate resources to fight the war that would also destroy the enemy's will to fight. Sherman intended to make Southerners' lives miserable; he argued it was more humane to take their property than

---

[164] Mahon, *The Shenandoah Valley*, 124-126.

their lives. As he succinctly stated, "War is hell." From November 15th to December 21st, 1864, Sherman, with 60,000 men, traveled 285 miles to Savannah, living off the land and covering a path up to 60 miles wide, reducing Georgia's midsection to debris and desolation. Men, known as bummers, a term for all army foragers, authorized or unauthorized, were ordered to forage and seize all Southern property that could be used in war and were responsible for most of the abuse. Not all abused their power, but many officers unsuccessfully attempted to stop those who did. Five thousand of Sherman's 60,000 men were assigned forage duties—50 men from each brigade. They were forbidden to enter occupied houses or burn houses without permission from higher authority, and they could only take what could be used for war, except for food. Sherman said they could take slaves but to be aware they had to feed them while living off the land.

Foragers would leave before daylight and proceed on foot five or six miles to visit every plantation, take what they confiscated, and meet the rest of the army on the route. One could never be sure what the bummers would bring back. One Union soldier commented that one bummer joined the main force riding a mule with a civilian saddle and a bed quilt and a blanket under it, carrying a bundle of fodder for the mule, three hams, a sack of flour, potatoes, a bed quilt, a coffee pot, a jug of vinegar, and a bedcord. He was followed by a squad of nearly two dozen bummers with chickens, geese, and beehives. One bummer brought a large hog strapped to his horse's back.

Foraging bummers committed many outrages. They searched every field, house, barn, and town, frequently vandalizing each home by ripping open feather beds, pillaging wardrobes and contents of chests, taking mirrors off walls, nabbing cooking utensils, and snatching quilts from beds. Widow Dolly Lunt, a resident of Georgia, vividly writes about her experiences when foragers came to her plantation: "Like demons they rushed in . . . to my smokehouse, my dairy, pantry, kitchen, and cellar, like famished wolves, they came breaking locks and whatever was in their way." A thousand pounds of meat was taken from the smokehouse. Numerous food items were also taken from the house. "My eighteen fat turkeys, my hens, my chickens and fowls, my young pigs, are shot down in my yard and hunted as if they were rebels themselves. I ran out and appealed to the guard," who responded, "I cannot help you, madam; it is orders." After a while, Sherman and the bulk of his men marched by Dolly's house, tearing down the garden paling to make a road through her "back yard and ... field driving their stock and riding through, tearing down her fences and desolating my home." Lunt's angst continued during the night.

> The two security guards came into my room and laid themselves by my fire for the night. I could not close my eyes but kept walking to and fro, watching the fires in the distance and dreading the approaching day, which, I feared, as they had not all passed, would be a continuation of horrors.

Even the slave cabins became victims of the bummers. They were "rifled of every valuable." Bummers, "to justify their actions, swore that slaves' Sunday clothes were the white's peoples' and that they never had money to get such things as they had."

A Georgia girl, Eliza Andrews, described that Georgia looked like the Yankees went through plundering houses and burning outbuilding, cotton, hay stacks, and fodder near Sparta, called the "Burnst Country" by residents.

> There was hardly a fence left standing . . . the fields were trampled down and the road was lined with carcasses of horses, hogs, and cattle that the invaders, unable to

consume or carry away with them, had wantonly shot down to starve the people and prevent them from making their crops. The stench in some places was unbearable: every hundred yards we had to hold our noses or stop them with cologne.

Confederate military forces under General Williams, Joseph Wheeler, Wade Hampton, and others attempted to thwart Sherman by engaging the Federals in combat, but their numbers were vastly inferior, and their attacks were ineffective.[165]

MARCHING THROUGH THE CAROLINAS

After reaching Savannah, Sherman went north into South Carolina, planning to eventually join Grant in Virginia. Railroads were among the primary targets. Disabling rail traffic to Virginia denied supplies to Lee. Sherman's men tore up the track and bent it around stumps and trees in shapes called "Sherman's Neckties." Sherman continued the devastation he inflicted upon Georgia but with greater vengeance and destruction because South Carolina had led the secession movement. Sherman's men marched through South Carolina, devastating a path 40 miles wide. Showing a vengeful attitude, bummers killed dogs and pups in an attempt to kill them all, in part because dogs were used for hunting down runaway slaves and roaming the fields of the plantation at night to keep the enslaved from running off. When a white lady protested the killing of her pups, she was told by bummers they would grow up to be dogs if they were not killed.[166]

Bummers crossing into North Carolina came across an unfortunate resident whom they robbed, taking his money, watch, and

---

[165] Henry Steele Commager, ed., *The Blue and Gray*, vol. 2 (New York: Bobbs-Merrill Company, 1950), 951-968.
[166] Boatner, *The Civil War Dictionary*, 512.

other valuables. Later the same day, another group came and shot him because he had nothing to steal. Southerners hid their food in the ground, hoping to avoid detection, but foragers found it by sticking ramrods of their muskets in the ground. Horses and cattle were driven into the swamps to save them, but Sherman's bummers would go "swamp ranging" looking for them. Not only were residents the victims of Yankee vandalism but Southern raiders, whom the victims hated the most.

All the homes bummers visited were ransacked, but the stately ones were significantly defaced. Bummers went into a beautiful home and rolled out an elegant piano in the yard, where they had carried valuable furniture, china, cut glass, old portraits, and other items precious to the family and chopped them up with axes. They rolled barrels of molasses and flour to parlors and poured the contents upon velvet carpets. Many homes were burned. They even took elderly citizens and hanged them until almost dead to force them to tell the bummers where their money was hidden. While moving through North Carolina, Sherman's men faced hard times from the lack of food and clothing. Many were barefooted, their clothes in tatters, forcing them to wear what they found foraging regardless of the color or cut. Some wore white vests, straw hats, and, occasionally, tails.[167]

In North Carolina, Sherman's army culled out one thousand unwanted and worthless horses and mules, herded them next to a river, and shot them. The bodies were left where they fell. A number floated down the river. In Fayetteville, Federals took all the horses they could not take with them and shot them in the street, leaving hundreds of dead horses that created an obnoxious odor despite the remains being burned.

---

[167] B. H. Liddell Hart, *Sherman* (New York: Da Capo Press, 1956), 346-347. Jerome Tew, "Ten Days of Hell: Sherman's Army in North Carolina," https://nccivilwarcenter.org>ten-days-of-hell-Sherman.

Sherman's March to the Sea and into the Carolinas had ransacked the "granary of the south," destroying rail traffic, leaving buildings plundered or in flames, and demolishing much of what was needed to sustain an agricultural society. Not the least was the loss of countless horses, mules, and other livestock. Along with Sherman's 60,000 men, he had 25,000 refugees; most were slaves from South Carolina, where burnings that included Columbia were more numerous than in North Carolina. For generations in the devastated areas, Sherman's name was connoted as a heartless villain, barbarian, vandal, and monster. Understandably, they did not see what Sherman claimed: that taking and destroying the enemies' property that supported their war effort was more humane than taking their lives. To the Southerners, what Sherman did was unforgivable.[168]

The war gravely impacted civilians, especially women, long before Sheridan burned the Shenandoah Valley and Sherman's March to the Sea. Colonel James C. Nisbet, a Georgian regiment commander, accurately stated, "It was upon women that the greatest burden of this war fell." The strain, anxiety, fear, loneliness, and hardships included the burden of grieving over the loss of a husband or son and being left with children without any means of support. Soon after secession, a woman from South Carolina lamented what was to come. "What do I care for patriotism? My husband is my country. What is my country to me if he be killed." No women suffered more than Confederate women of the yeoman class, and none reflects their desperation more than a letter from a wife to her husband stationed with Lee's army in Virginia in 1862, pleading for him to come home. Upon reading her description of their son crying out in the night from the pangs of hunger, their young daughter growing thinner every day, and Mary writing, "And before God, Edward, unless you come home, we must die," he deserted. The letter was used in

---

[168] Richard Wheeler, *Sherman's March* (New York: Thomas Y. Crowell,1978) 24. 109-120, 173-174.

his defense during his court-martial in December 1862. Edward was found guilty, but Lee pardoned him and had him report for duty. Letters like Mary's accelerated in number as the war continued, with thousands deserting and Lee pointing out they "severely weakened his army."

CHAPTER 10

COMPANIONS IN MISERY

In many ways, war animals' military life parallels the problems soldiers endure, such as exhaustion and fatigue, hunger, heat, cold, illness and disease, parasites, wounds, and death.

THE DEADLIEST FOE

For the soldier, disease was the deadliest foe. The same was valid for horses and mules. The Union Army had more than a million and a half men, and the Confederates had a little over a million. Traditionally, it was believed approximately 620,000 were killed during the Civil War: 360,000 Union and 260,000 Confederates. Today, the number is approximately 750,000 total lives lost, which means the Civil War claims a greater number of deaths than the combined deaths in all other wars in which America has currently participated in. Three out of five of the Federal deaths were from disease, and for the Confederates, it was two out of three. During the first year of the war, one-third of the Union Army was on sick call. It was probably worse for the Confederates. Leading the list of deadly diseases were diarrhea and dysentery, typhoid, and inflammation of the lungs. Some men lingered and suffered for months before they died. During the war, around 94,000 Confederates and 110,000 Union soldiers died from battle wounds, most inflicted by the rifle-musket.[169]

When the Civil War began, there were 4,688,678 horses in the Northern states and 2,800,000 in the Southern. The loss of horses and mules during the war was enormous. It is estimated that between 1,200,000 and 1,500,000 horses and mules died in military service; like the soldiers, most died of disease. Of humans, one-third were killed in combat, and two-thirds died from disease. Although there are no records of the causes and numbers of deaths of horses, it is estimated that one-tenth of the horses died from battle wounds and nine-tenth from sickness and disease.[170]

Factors hindering the survival of humans and animals were the tardiness of both combatants in providing medical care and the backwardness of knowledge and treatment. The surgeon general of the United States, Thomas Lawson, considered it foolish to buy medical textbooks, and Union General Don Carlos Buell did not believe in having a medical corp. The attitude of many was that the purpose of war was to tear bodies apart, not mend them. There were 33,000 physicians in the United States at the start of the war, and more than 12,000 served on both sides; most had two years of medical school. Physicians of the era did not understand that germs were microscopic organisms that caused disease.[171] This is indicated by the lack of cleanliness of Civil War surgeons, many of whom had never seen an operation before the war. They rarely washed their hands, used their fingers to remove a Minié ball, and wiped their instruments on their blood-stained aprons. They had no concern that their

---

169 Stewart Brooks, *Civil War Medicine*, (Springfield, Illinois: Charles C. Thomas Publisher, 1966), 4-7. Browning and Silver, *An Environmental History of the Civil War*, 136.
170 Heiss, *Veterinary Service During the American Civil War*, 33, 54.
171 Susan Beller, *Medical Practices in the Civil War*, (Published by Susan Beller, 1992), 19, 21.

instruments were dirty as long as they were sharp and cut well. After surgery, the appearance of pus was not considered an indication of an infection but a good thing, a sign of healing.[172]

Veterinarian medicine was in its infancy and, with few veterinarians, horses and mules were primarily cared for by farriers. Like the care for soldiers, both sides were slow in addressing the medical needs of equines. Midway through the war, both sides established depots like Giesboro to rehabilitate equines.[173]

Diarrhea and dysentery were the leading killers of soldiers. The highly contagious glanders would occupy that slot for horses and mules. Glanders attacks mucous membranes and lymphatic systems in infected animals. There is no cure. It is passed easily to other animals by a sick animal by simply being among them. Symptoms include high fevers, a thick nasal discharge, and ulceration of the nose. Death usually occurs within a few days after symptoms appear.[174]

HUNGER

The lack of food for men and animal feed became a more significant problem for Confederates than for the Union, which had superior resources. But at times, it was a problem for both. Almost every regiment had to endure occasional hunger for a few days, but there were also periods of prolonged shortages involving large numbers of men. Food shortages were most common when the armies were moving and during combat.

In the West, early in 1862, there were many instances of prolonged hunger. Rations were short for the Union soldiers in late 1862

---

172 Ibid.
173 Hess, *Animals Histories of the Civil War*, 58-59.
174 Heiss, *Veterinary Service During the American Civil War*, 54, 77.

in the Kentucky Campaign, forcing men to rob horse troughs of hard corn to eat. Others complained they only had three crackers to eat for ten days.

During the Valley Campaign of 1862, General Fremont's Union troops were destitute, causing Carl Schurz to inform Lincoln of their situation: "The government has plenty of provisions, and our soldiers die of hunger; plenty of shoes, and they go barefooted, plenty of horses, and we can hardly move."[175] That November and December under General Burnside at Fredericksburg was the first general food shortage of the second winter of the war. Men begged for hard bread and picked up heads, feet, and tails from slaughtered steers for food. A soldier wrote home: "I must fall in for my beans or lose them. We have two beans to a pint of water."[176] General Hooker replaced Burnside in January 1863 and brought about a revolution in providing food. Hooker's reforms included the erection of bakeries to give soft bread to men and improved supply lines. As a result of the reforms, except for brief shortages, the Army of the Potomac fared well during the summer and fall of 1863 until November during the Mine Run Campaign.

The western armies had a greater food shortage, especially during 1862 and early 1863, due to the lack of efficiency by supply officials and their failure to distribute food meant for soldiers by diverting it for their use. Few soldiers could afford to buy food from the sutlers, but they foraged, occasionally had meals with civilians, mainly the enslaved, and eagerly received food from their families back home.[177] But this was not enough to meet their needs.

---

175 Brooks, *Civil War Medicine*, 9. Heiss, *Veterinary Service During the American Civil War*, 73-76.
176 Bell Irvin Wiley, *The Life of Billy Yank* (New York: Bobbs-Merrill Company, 1952), 226.
177 Ibid.

For Sherman's men in the March to the Sea and movement in South and North Carolina, it was feast or famine. Especially in Savannah and northern South Carolina, not enough food was raised by foraging. In his diary, one soldier lamented his spare meal of a cracker and a cup of coffee.[178]

The Confederates' food shortages were like the Union's in that they were worse during troop movement and campaigning. Shortages for the Confederates got worse as the war went on, not because of a shortage of food production but because of poor distribution due to an inadequate rail system, poor financing, the shrinking Confederacy, and the lack of salt as a preservative. The Confederate government's official rations for soldiers were constantly reduced throughout the war. This doomed the Southern warriors to four years of primarily eating cornbread and bad beef.

Food shortages struck early in the war for the Confederates in July 1861, a week after the Battle of First Manassas (First Battle of Bull Run); General Beauregard wrote Jefferson Davis not to send any more troops to Virginia because some regiments were near starvation. Confederate winters in Kentucky were even worse. Lard was used as a substitute for bacon; the meat was so tough, the colonel threatened to order files to sharpen the men's teeth, and starving livestock chewed on wagons, halters, bridle reins, and stumps. A desperate mule attempted to eat a horse's tail. This was a far cry from what equines needed. An average cavalry force of 1,000 horses needed seven tons of hay and six tons of grain daily. Large herds soon stripped grass around camps of vegetation, and that offered only a temporary solution.

As the war continued, food shortages for the Confederates became worse. The unusually severe winter of 1864-1865

---
178   Ibid., 225-235.

increased the suffering of man and beast. Things were desperate. A Confederate soldier, Alexander Hunter, later wrote: "To say that the Army of Northern Virginia was literally on the verge of starvation was telling nothing but the woeful, pathetic truth." Rations were reduced, so they barely kept soldiers alive.[179] At Appomattox in April 1865, a private found that all the food for his division had been eaten when applying for a meal. He was given two ears of corn on the cob for the horses. The soldier cooked the corn in coals and added salt. It was not easy to eat. Chewing the corn was hard work, making the jaw ache and the gums and teeth sore.[180]

The suffering of the infantry was great, but the condition of cavalry and artillery was even worse. Seeing animals with loose hides hanging over bony frames was sad. Many were too weak to pull a wagon. The ration of corn and fodder was not even a third of what they needed. Troopers and artillerymen were so famished, that they were given half of the corn intended for the horses. To help alleviate this plight, cavalrymen were sent home for the winter to lessen the strain on the commissary. Only three companies out of a brigade were sent away to recuperate and return in the spring. Unfortunately for the Confederates, this provided only temporary relief.

The South was running out of other resources as well. In the last year of the war, they were short of ammunition, forcing them to cut and burn trees around Richmond where battles had been fought to get bullets lodged in them. Not only did Lee's men look physically worn, but they looked like beggars by the time they got to the Appomattox Court House, with holes and patches everywhere, covered with dirt and mud, and wearing all sorts of costumes because of

---

179 Henry Steele Commageer, ed., *The Blue and the Gray* 951-959. Hunter, *Johnny Reb and Billy Yank*, 663-665. T. Glatthaar, *The March to the Sea and Beyond* (Baton Rouge: Louisiana State University Press, 1985), 131. Bell Irvin Wiley, *The Life of Johnny Reb* (New York: Bobbs-Merrill Company, 1943), 90-98.
180 Browning and Silver, *An Environmental History of the Civil War*, 109. Richard Wheeler, *Witness to Appomattox* (New York: Harper & Row, 1989), 147.

the shortage of uniforms. They wore anything that would keep rain and cold from their bony bodies, including headgear that was rarely seen. One officer led a Confederate charge wearing a lawyer's gown and a woman's hat tied over a woolen nightcap.[181]

When Lee surrendered, his army had dwindled to 29,000 starving men. Among them was John Kees, a 54th Regiment South Carolina infantry member. After surrendering, he and several others walked back to Wilkes County, North Carolina, without food. On their way home, they came across a peach tree with small, immature fruit. They were so famished they stripped the tree bare, but Kees said the best thing he had was a field mouse. He cooked it and ate it all, hair and entrails.[182]

WEATHER

Extreme weather, including heat, cold, rain, and snow, adversely affected soldiers, horses, and mules, as did the consequences of extreme weather, droughts, floods, and mud. Weather was a significant factor in the failure of Confederates to gain control of New Mexico and Arizona due to the scarcity of grass and water. The Battle of Valverde, New Mexico, on February 21st, 1862, was over the region's primary water source: the Rio Grande River, held by Union forces. Confederates were desperate for water and risked capture crawling through Union lines to fill their canteens. Confederate horses and mules suffered terribly and gave out cries of anguish. Many mules broke away in search of water and were captured by the Union.

The lack of water was the primary concern of Confederate and Union soldiers as they approached the Battle of Perryville, Kentucky, in October 1862. The only available water was stagnant and putrid,

---

[181] Hunter, *Johnny Reb and Billy Yank*, 665.
[182] Johnson J. Hayes, *The Land of Wilkes* (Wilkesboro, North Carolina: Wilkes County Historical Society, 1962), 490."

and guards had to be placed around them to keep men from drinking the sickening water. The Battle of Perryville started as the result of the conflict for water. On October 7th, Federal soldiers drove away Southern forces at Doctor's Creek, a small stream made up of mud holes. Still, the Confederates desired the nearly stagnant water and counter-attacked the next day, and the Battle of Perryville was on.

The lack of rain and increased demand for water by large military forces led to a shortage of drinking water at Antietam and Vicksburg. A month after the start of the Siege of Vicksburg, cisterns, old wells, and those recently dug by Confederate soldiers could not meet the fivefold increased need for water. Confederates found the water from the Mississippi created another problem: sickness. The water was contaminated with human waste and dead animals.

At the close of the First Battle of Bull Run on July 12th, 1861, Union forces, exhausted by a long day of marching and fighting, were further debilitated by dehydration, which the men called "sun struck." The heat significantly reduced their numbers. Some companies were left with only eight men.

Flooding made the Union's capture of Fort Henry on February 6th, 1862, easier. The Tennessee River was 30 feet above flood stage, and it flooded the powder magazines at the fort, denying Confederates adequate ammunition. Rain also helped Grant in his victory at Shiloh in the spring of 1862. It delayed the Confederates' plan to launch an attack for two days, allowing Grant to receive reinforcements. After the battle, the Confederates retreated to Corinth amidst rain, sleet, and mud that was shoe-top deep. The contaminated water made soldiers sick, and they had to endure the sweet, sickening stench of decaying human and horse bodies uncovered by the pelting rain. Rain plagued George McClellan, slowing his movement toward Richmond during the Peninsular Campaign in the spring of 1862. Thirteen days of rain made the movement of both sides difficult, with suffering, struggling, exhausted men marching through deep mud, burning calories that far exceeded that provided by their food, causing Union and Confederate soldiers to collapse.

Frigid cold weather hindered the retreat of Jeb Stuart's men in late 1861 in northern Virginia back to their Confederate winter camp at Centreville, 20 miles away. In the cold darkness, weary men with sore feet traveled on hard, frozen ground. Each moved slowly the best they could, suffering from the cold as they arrived the next day at their camp. Almost two days after the Battle of Dranesville, which started when the two sides clashed while foraging for hay, corpses from the battlefield were frozen in the posture of their death when they arrived at Centreville; some lay doubled up while others' rigid fingers clutched their clothing or accouterments.[183]

Cold, ice, snow, and rain inflicted great suffering on Stonewall Jackson's men during the Romney Expedition in the first two weeks of 1862. The mission was to kick out Federals who occupied Romney and beyond (now West Virginia) and secure the area to the east, which included Winchester, Virginia. The weather was warm when Jackson's men left Winchester, so they discarded their coats. After a few days, the temperature dropped at night and plunged to eight degrees, causing the soles of shoes to freeze to the ground as bad frozen roads covered with snow and ice made travel extremely difficult—and led to extensive straggling. One Confederate recorded, "Getting up grade was somewhat like the frog's climbing out of the well, for every step forward we slipped two back. We never would have made progress but for the fact that when marching down hill we made up by slipping three feet forward for every step we took."

---

[183] Browning and Silver, *An Environmental History of the Civil War,* 447, 57-58, 67-68, 99-100. Charles P. Poland Jr., *The Glories of War* (Blooming, Indiana: AuthorHouse, 2006), 73-74, 187-188.

Kid Douglas vividly describes the experience in *I Rode with Stonewall*:

> Rain, snow, and storm spent their fury upon the unprotected troops, at one time marching through water, mud, and slush and again over hill and valley of solid ice. Sometimes, it was impossible for men of a regiment to move together over the smooth roads, and limbs were broken, as well as guns and swords when a dozen men went down at the same time. Sometimes a team of four would be struggling on the ice, while the wagon or artillery to which they were attached was pressing upon them, slipping over the glassy surface ... I have not been able to find any man in the 2nd Reg. who did not fall down at least twice.

Falling on the ice killed several horses. They were unable to pull wagons because they lacked winter shoes and needed to be "ice calked," where nail-like iron wedges were added to the hooves for better traction. "Icicles of blood hung from horses" due to their falls. On two occasions, Jackson dismounted to put his shoulder on a wagon to keep it from slipping backward. This gesture had little impact on his men's attitude. They blamed him for their plight, cursed him, and repeatedly muttered, Jackson is insane."[184]

A year after Jackson's Romney Expedition, excessive rain thwarted Union General Ambrose Burnside. His army suffered extensive losses at the Battle of Fredericksburg in the fall of 1862. After the battle, he attempted to get behind Lee by crossing the Rappahannock River at Bank's Ford, ignoring that rain had made the roads impassable. The march, known as the Mud March, started on January 21st, 1862, amidst heavy rain. One participant lamented, "The feet of men and animals, the wheels of guns, caisson, limber,

---

[184] James I. Robertson Jr, *Stonewall Jackson* (New York: Macmillan Publishing, 1997), 311.

and wagon" were held so tight that 12 horses could not move a gun, and men frequently stopped to rest after going a short distance. It had to be challenging even for the dogs accompanying the Federals. "The wheels of vehicles disappeared entirely. On January 20th, Union forces with pontoons, vehicles, hundreds of horses, and mules were mired in the mud as Confederates had arrived first at Bank's Ford across the river holding tautening signs."[185] The movement had failed; how could the Union soldiers return to the camp? The retreat started on January 23rd over the same roads their movement to the ford had destroyed, taking some men until January 26th to return to camp. Lincoln soon replaced Burnside with "Fighting Joe Hooker."[186]

The Mud March (Library of Congress)

---

185   Douglas, *I Rode With Stonewall*, 33. Robertson Jr., *Stonewall Jackson*, 308-311, 844.
186   Donald, *Divided We Fought*, 148. "The Mud March" <u>https://www.nps.gov>articles>mudmarch</u>.

COMBAT

Over ten thousand fights occurred during the Civil War, totaling 10,455 military actions. They include 29 campaigns, 76 battles, and thousands of lesser conflicts listed as engagements, combat, actions, skirmishes, affairs, and other names. The distinction between them is vague at best.[187] For the soldier wounded or killed, the size of the battle did not matter. The danger and fear of being a casualty and the pain and agony of being wounded were the same.

Battles frequently started with thundering, deafening artillery fire to soften up the enemy before an infantry charge. The unsuspecting noise startled bewildered wildlife. Two hundred and thirty bird species inhabited the military theaters during the Civil War. Usually, they flew about peacefully, observed by the soldiers below, but deafening artillery fire led to erratic behavior. A Union reporter at the Battle of Murfreesboro reported the following about flocks of sparrows:

> [Sparrows] fluttered and circled above the field in a state of utter bewilderment, and scores of rabbits fled for protection to our men and lying down inline on the left, nestling under their coats and creeping under their legs in a state of utter distraction. They hopped over the field like toads and as perfectly tamed by fright as household pets.[188]

Wildlife and domestic animals became innocent victims of battlefield fire. After the first day of fighting at the Second Battle of Bull Run at Brawner's Farm in late August 1862, all the farm animals were dead in their pens and in the field of the battle were dead birds and rabbits.[189]

---

187 E. B. Long, *The Civil War Day by Day* (New York: Doubleday & Company, 1971), 719.
188 Wiley, *The Life of Billy Yank*, 80.
189 Hess, *Animal Histories of the Civil War Era*, 73. Alan D. Gaff, *Brave Men's Tears* (Dayton, Ohio: Morningside House, 1988), 178.

WOUNDS

During combat, horses and mules were especially vulnerable. They were larger than men and were a larger target. Horses were often struck by bullets intended for the rider. A Union artilleryman, John Billings, found the horse's combat behavior superior to men's, calling the response of equines to wounds "heroism." Horses often made no noise when receiving a wound, but where they were hit determined how they reacted. Some wounds led to squeals of pain and erratic movement. Bullets that struck the horse in the leg made a snapping sound, and the horse fell to the ground. When a bullet hits the fleshy part of an animal, it sounds like a pebble thrown in the mud. Some horses became unmanageable and ran off, running over foot soldiers and injuring them, but most did not. Unlike a few soldiers, who faked being wounded and retreated, horses often continue to function. Billings saw one horse shot in the neck, but it "had no more effect than shake his head as if pestered by a fly." Billing also saw Union General Winfield Scott Hancock's horse during a battle receive a wound in the neck, causing him to fall and appear dead. The general mounted another horse, but the wounded horse "arose and shook himself, was at once remounted by the general, and survived the war many years."

Artillery horses were prime targets of the enemy. Billings stated, "It seemed sad to see a single horse standing, with his five companions all lying dead or dying around him, himself the object of a concentration of fire until the fatal shot laid him low." On one occasion, Billings saw one horse struck by bullets seven times before it died. In one battle, Billings noted that only four of their 57 artillery horses had survived. When close enough, cavalrymen used their sabers on horses and mules to immobilize wagons.[190]

---

190   Billings, *Hardtack and Coffee*, 327-328.

RELUCTANT PARTICIPANTS

Union artillery horses killed on Trostle Farm on July 2nd, 1863 (*Battles and Leaders of the Civil War Vol. 3*)

On the second day of the Battle of Shiloh in April 1862, Grant and two of his staff came under fire. They did not realize Colonel McPherson's horse was hit. When they had ridden to safety, the horse was panting and looked like it was about to collapse. On examining the mount, they found a bullet had struck him in the flank back of the saddle and gone through. In a matter of minutes, the horse dropped dead, having given no sign of injury until they came to a stop.[191] One of the more gruesome sights which occurred at Shiloh was when a wounded horse galloped between the lines, snorting in terror as his entrails, full of dirt and dust, trailed behind him.[192]

Dogs followed their men into combat and suffered heavy casualties. Of the 21 dogs listed in Michael Zucchero's *Loyal Hearts*, 5 were killed; 9 others were injured, some several times. Some

---

191   Ulysses S. Grant, *Personal Memoirs of U. S. Grant* (New York: J. Little and Co., 1885), vol. 1, 353-354.
192   Armistead, *Horses and Mules in the Civil War*, 42..

survived injuries from accidents outside the battlefield, like Curly, who belonged to an Ohio infantry unit and fell off a railcar. Less fortunate was Charlie, who belonged to the Ohio infantrymen and participated in 15 major engagements from April 19th, 1861. He was killed in combat near Farmville, Virginia, on April 7th, 1865, two days before Lee's surrender.

Sallie, the 11th Pennsylvania Infantry mascot, followed men into numerous battles and was wounded in one. At Gettysburg, she licked the wounded and stood guard over the dead. She was killed by a bullet to the head at the Battle of Hatcher's Run in February 1865. The small dog is memorialized by a life-size sculpture at the base of the 11th Pennsylvania monument on the Gettysburg battlefield. She became one of the most famous Civil War dogs.

Union Captain Werner Von Bachelle became inseparable from a Newfoundland dog that wandered into his camp. The animal followed his master into battle, including the bloody battle at Antietam, where Von Bachelle was killed in Miller's cornfield. The dog would not leave despite the heavy fire from cannons, rifle fire, and calls from Bachelle's comrades. Two days later, their bodies were found, the dog's across his master's.[193]

Many gruesome scenes of course involved wounded soldiers. An example was a wound sustained by Lieutenant A. H. Cushing of the Union artillery at Gettysburg on July 3rd, 1863, as Confederates in Pickett's Charge temporarily breached the Federal line. The 22-year-old Cushing was struck in the crotch by an exploding shell. His second wound tore open his abdomen and groin, exposing his intestines and requiring him to hold his internal organs in with one hand. While in agony, he attempted to retain command. But he was

---

[193] Anne Palagruto, *Civil War Dogs and the Men Who Loved Them* (no publisher or date), 21-23, 39. Zucchero, *Loyal Hearts*, 147-150.

too weak to yell orders that could be heard. He was held up by a sergeant who passed on Cushing's orders. A short time after his second wound, he was killed when a bullet entered his mouth and exited through the back of his skull.[194]

Likewise emotionally moving was Captain Spessard at Pickett's Charge with his son, who was killed. Soldiers around him saw the father kiss the body tenderly and lay his son gently on the ground, then raise his sword and continue the charge.[195] More fortunate was Confederate General John Brown Gordon, who was wounded five times during the war but lived until his death in 1890. He was severely wounded in the head at "Bloody Lane" during the Battle of Antietam. He fell forward unconscious, and if there had not been a hole in his cap, he would have drowned in his blood.[196]

After a battle, the most pressing need for both combatants was to care for the wounded; in large battles, thousands of wounded men were scattered about over a large area. They were taken to temporary makeshift hospitals in a field, barn, or house where they went under a surgeon's knife, then were later moved to one of the permanent hospitals. An example of the need for immediate care is the aftermath of the Battle of Antietam. The Union had just under 10,000 wounded at Antietam, and in seeking temporary hospitals, they had to spread out the wounded in structures over approximately 75 miles.

---

194 George R. Stewart, *Pickett's Charge* (Dayton, Ohio: Morningside Bookshop. 1983), 157-158.
195 Ezra J. Warner, *Generals in Gray* (Batton Rouge: Louisianna State Press, 1959), 111.
196 Ibid.

Temporary Union hospital in a field after the Battle of Antietam. Muskets and bayonets were used as tent poles. (Library of Congress)

Confederate Alexander Hunter described his experience after being wounded in the leg during the Battle of the Wilderness in May 1864. He was found the night after the battle, cold, lying on the ground in a pool of his own blood, with his leg swollen twice its normal size. He was taken to the yard of the Culpeper Court House. He lay there until the next day with hundreds of other unattended wounded soldiers. Finally, he was taken to the top floor of the courthouse. Hunter said the following of his treatment:

> [It was a] homeopathic plan . . . that was the only one our doctors followed, whether they believed in it or not. Cold water was plentiful, and with no other restoring agent at hand, they all became advocates of the cold-water cure. All the wounded were treated alike . . . Their wounds were bandaged with a handful of lint, over which was a bandage of cotton; the canteen of water was placed in a patient's hand, that he might keep the cloth always wet . . . There were more than a hundred cavalrymen lying in one room, and the odor and the gathering of flies made the place like a charnel [bone] house.

Later in the evening, several surgeons, who had been on their feet for 48 hours, arrived, and limbs were taken off in the next room. "The frightful noise of saw searing bone was plainly audible. The dead were removed," and the survivors were cared for. The following day, 15 more men died, and their bodies were removed.

Alexander Hunter witnessed many deaths.

> There is a horrible fascination in watching dying men; turn your eyes which way you will, they will invariably return to those whose sands of life are nearly run out. You can count the gasping breath, behold the spasmodic clutching at the air, the respiration getting fainter and taken at long intervals, the glazing eye, the blackening lips. The shy pallor of the face, and at last the rattling of the throat and the convulsive shuddering of their limbs as the immortal spirit leaves its tenement of clay."[197]

One of the most heart-touching stories of the war occurred at Chimborazo Hospital in Richmond, one of the better, more permanent Confederate care centers due to the excellent work of the matron Phoebe Yates Pember. One of the patients was a young man

---

197 Hunter, *Johnny Reb and Billy Yank*, 547-551, 557.

who was gentle and uncomplaining and a favorite of the hospital staff. He had received a severe leg wound ten months earlier and was finally able to walk with crutches.

But one night, the wound started bleeding. They assumed it was from the sharp edge of a splintered bone that severed an artery. Pember pressed her finger on the wound to stop the bleeding and waited for the surgeon, who shook his head upon examination, finding the artery too deeply buried in the flesh for him to do anything. Pember had the unenviable task of telling the young man, who had no idea of his condition. He received the devastating news courageously and asked Pember, "How long can I live?" The matron informed him only as long as she kept her finger on the artery. After a long silence, he told her she could let go, but she could not as tears rushed to her eyes and a pounding filled her ears. But the decision was made for her—she fainted.[198]

Some of the most eerie and tragic scenes were the aftermath of a large battle. The night after was especially so. Numerous sounds of misery and pain dominated the night air. Wounded and dying horses made pitiful sounds of desperation, some often struggling in failed attempts to stand. Lantern-carrying litter-bearers walked among the dead, searching for the wounded to take to overworked surgeons who sawed off damaged limbs and gave what aid they could to those beyond saving. Among the thousands of injured, there were too many to gather immediately. Many were left in darkness on the battlefield, where they called for water, a loved one back home, or help. Some quietly endured their agony and waited for help or death to end their pain. With ill intent, others searched through the pants and coat pockets of the vulnerable stricken forms lying on the ground, ghoulishly robbing them of anything of value.

---

[198] Bell I. Wiley, editor, *A Southern Woman's Story* (Jackson Tennessee: McCowat-Mercer Press, 1959), 66-68.

There were almost endless other horrors faced on the battlefield. One was the danger of the wounded being burned alive in the Battle of the Wilderness. Fires broke out in the wooded battlefield that trapped immobile wounded; some were unable to escape. The wounded capped their weapons, ready to take their life if the flames reached them.

Wounded trapped in the fire during the Battle of the Wilderness (*Harper's Weekly*)

A number of men were killed when they attempted to disarm shells at the Siege of Vicksburg. Unfortunately, a small black child was playing with an unexploded shell and pounded on the fuse, which exploded, destroying the youth. The destruction of Vicksburg left a battle area Confederate Sergeant Willie Tunnard described as hell.

> Houses dilapidated and in ruins . . . fences pulled down, and houses pulled to pieces for firewood . . . wagons parked in graveyards, horses trampled down graves, and

men using tombstones as convenient tables for scanty meals . . . Dogs howled through the streets at night; cats screamed forth their hideous cries; an army of rats, seeking food, would scamper around your feet and across the streets and over the pavement, lice, and filth covered the bodies of soldiers.

Half-starved horses subsisting on cane tops and mulberry leaves were in constant fear from artillery. One account of horses fastened to trees shows just how full of terror they were.

[The horses would] strain the halter to its full length, rearing high in the air with a loud snort of terror, as a shell would explode near. I could hear them, in the night, cry out in the midst of an uproar, ending in a low, plaintive whinny of fear.[199]

A moving, blood-stained letter of a dying Confederate soldier, J.R. Montgomery of Mississippi, reveals the presence of mind to write one last letter to his father after a shell struck his right shoulder, leaving it horribly mangled on May 10th, 1864, at Spotsylvania, Virginia. He informed his father he was weak and knew death was inevitable but thought he would be delighted to hear from his dying son. A friend would write him about the particulars of his son's death. Montogomery expressed a wish to be buried at home with his mother and brothers, but he would leave it up to his father. He had prayed to God He would forgive him of his sins and closed with a touching goodbye. "A long farewell to you. May we meet in heaven. Your dying son, J. R. Montgomery." He lingered four more days.

---

[199] Edward J. Stackpole, *From Cedar Mountain to Antietam* (Harrisburg, Pennsylvania: The Stackpole Company, 1959), 437. Wheeler, *The Siege of Vicksburg*, 197, 223.

THE PSYCHOLOGICALLY WOUNDED

Some were free from physical harm but suffered psychological damage. Today, this is known as PTSD and is rampant among recent veterans with an alarming suicide rate. The nature and trauma of war, which is the antithesis of behavior accepted in peaceful, civilized society, leaves psychological wounds that make living in the aftermath of war difficult, and for some, unbearable, as they suffer from depression, flashbacks, sleeplessness, and other torturous maladies. The symptoms of the psychologically wounded have been the same throughout history, but the name has changed. Even the Egyptians, Romans, and Greeks were aware of soldiers who were psychologically injured. It was called Da Costa's syndrome after a doctor who studied 300 soldiers during the Civil War and immediately after. This was followed by "soldier's heart." During World War I, it was referred to as "shell shock." In World War II, it was called "combat fatigue," and today, it is known as PTSD (post-traumatic stress disorder). Treatment in the past was scant and ineffective. Today, canine therapy is one avenue of treatment for this illness. One of the retarding influences in providing treatment is the belief that soldiers who show the symptoms of PTSD (depression, sleeplessness, flashbacks, paranoia, and violent behavior) are weak and potentially deserters looking for some way to escape their duties as soldiers.

Can war and stress cause animals to commit suicide? The belief that animals commit suicide has been popular since the 19th century. However, the issue was addressed over 2,000 years ago by the Greeks. They seemed to think so. This view anthropomorphizes animals, giving them the attributes of humans, such as motivation and consciousness. It has not been proven that animals commit suicide, although some behave in a way that seems suicidal, such as refusing to eat when stressed or grieving. Some social insects have been known to sacrifice themselves to defend their colony.

Another animal whose behavior seems suicidal is the small, sensitive Tarsier, weighing 30 grams, which lives in the Philippines and islands in the Pacific Ocean. Tarsiers are super sensitive to light and noise, and being touched stresses them out. They will bash their thin skulls against trees, floors, and cage walls, which frequently leads to their death.[200]

Academics conclude that "animal suicide is when an animal intentionally ends its life through its action." Experts have been very wary of ascribing a wide range of cognitive capacities to nonhuman animals, such as the concept of self, death, and future intention. They accept that they have emotions and that stress can alter their lives. In the Civil War, numerous dogs were traumatized by their master's death, refusing to leave their bodies. One dog stayed on the spot where his master was killed long after his master's body was removed; people nearby brought him food to keep him from starving.[201]

BURIAL OF THE DEAD

Demanding immediate resolution at the end of a battle after caring for the wounded was the burial of the dead. For humans, this process was twofold. The first was a temporary burial on the battlefield, and the second was the movement of the remains to more permanent sites, often occurring years later. Many of the dead's identities are not known because Civil War soldiers did not have dog tags. The temporary burials were often in shallow graves, and rain and animals soon exposed parts of the body. The lack of burials was especially true when buried by the enemy, who had far less concern for those who were trying to kill them than when burying someone on their side.

---

200 Rebecca Frankel, *War Dogs* (New York: St. Martin's Press, 2015), 190-191.
201 "Animal Suicide," Wikipedia (https://en.wikipedia.org>wiki>Animals_suicide. "Do Animals Commit Suicide?" https://www.magazine.com>Planet Earth.

DEAD IN THE "WHEAT-FIELD" GATHERED FOR
BURIAL. FROM PHOTOGRAPHS.

Dead on the Gettysburg Battlefield (*Battles and Leaders of the Civil War Vol. 3*)

Burial of Confederate dead at Gettysburg (*Battles and Leaders of the Civil War Vol. 3*)

At Fox's Gap, in the preliminary fighting before the Battle of Antietam, the Union crammed Confederate dead down a well next to the dwelling because it was easier than digging graves. Animal and human corpses deteriorated rapidly in the sun and heat. Human bodies became black and bloated in a matter of hours, tearing through their clothing and often rupturing, emitting stomach-turning odors that sickened those on burial detail. A sickly-sweet smell of putrefaction was emitted for a month or more for unburied carcasses. Bayonets were made into hooks to snag the clothing of the dead and drag them to a spot with other dead without having to touch the reeking remains. Other burial parties used shovels to move the decaying corpses. Embalming was rare on the battlefront and usually only for some officers. A few bodies were shipped home by rail, wagon, or stagecoach, where transport personnel had to deal with the intolerable aroma. The human dead were buried in single graves or large trenches like at Andersonville and Vicksburg. Burial trenches at Vicksburg were smaller than Andersonville's at 50 feet long and three feet wide, usually accommodating eight bodies. Andersonville needed a larger trench to accommodate the 100 or more men who died daily during August 1864.

Andersonville cemetery (Library of Congress)

On some battlegrounds, corpses were buried in single graves. The grave was dug as close to the body as possible, and the remains were rolled into it. Most would be later moved to permanent grave sites. Of the 360,222 Union soldier deaths, 110,100 were killed in battle. Those selected for burial detail were prisoners of war or those being punished for straggling or other violations. A significant number of the Union fatalities are buried in 14 national cemeteries. There were 258,000 Confederate deaths, and 94,000 were the result of combat. The remains of Confederates are scattered over 250 cemeteries, mainly in the South. Anger from the Union's neglect of the Confederate dead ignited a movement in Southern Memorial Association, who called to bring their dead back home. In 1872, 279 plain wooden boxes containing the remains of 708 Confederates killed at Gettysburg arrived in Richmond for reinterment in Hollywood Cemetery. Only 239 of the remains were identified. They were placed in single boxes. As many as 12 unknowns were put together in larger containers. The cost was $3.24 to disinter, box, and ship each body to Richmond. The Federals began moving 3,534 Union Gettysburg dead to the new Soldier's National Cemetery in the middle of the battlefield in the fall of 1863. It took five months to complete the project. At the dedication on November 19th, 1863, Lincoln made his famous Gettysburg Address. The federal government spent four million dollars removing and reinterring Union dead from the South. Like the South, which was upset with the Federals' treatment of Southern bodies, the Union was upset with the South's disregard for Union dead that were often on top of the ground and eaten by hogs.[202]

---

202   Browning and Silver, *An Environmental History of the Civil War,* 136-137. Hess, *Animal Histories of the Civil War Era,* 144. Mary H. Mitchell, *Hollywood Cemetery* (Virginia State Library, Richmond, 1985), 83-92.

Removing the carcasses of the large number of horses killed presented a problem. Their bodies were much larger than soldiers' and were just as unsavory. The battlefield was covered with swollen and decaying horses and mules, some with body parts scattered about by exploding shells. Many horses died soon after being wounded. Others had a lingering death. After receiving what was perceived as a fatal wound, many were turned loose to die and often sadly attempted to follow other horses. Others were shot. The horses killed in the Battle of Fair Oaks outside of Richmond in 1862 were burned. This became a common practice, as did leaving horse and mule carcasses to decay above ground, their bones bleaching in the sun. Others were buried, and an ax was used to break the legs that would stick out of the ground. The stench was so foul, whether burying men or equines, members of the burial detail became sick and threw up.

The burning of horse carcasses and the burial of human dead after the Battle of Fair Oaks in 1862 (Library of Congress)

The repulsive smell of decaying corpses made the men of the burial detail sick. The ax was to break the legs of a horse being buried. (John D. Billings, *Hardtack and Coffee*)

Horses and mules that could be rehabilitated in the latter part of the war were shot to prevent them from falling into Confederate hands. Contagious animals that died in corrals were dumped in the Potomac, Mississippi, and smaller rivers and streams, in hopes they would wash out to sea. Instead, they collected along riverbanks, creating an unhealthy and putrid environment. At Giesboro outside Washington, where 300 horses died daily, an expensive 40-man crew was busy burying dead equines. To reduce the cost, animal carcasses and manure from the corral were sold to private individuals who profited by turning a $2 investment for carcasses into $6 by selling body parts: hide, tallow, bones, hooves, and tail. In 1864 and 1865, agents of companies went to major battle sites and purchased the bones of burned carcasses of horses and mules, paying 50 cents per one hundred pounds. Individuals who lived on farms that became battlefields had to get rid of dead animal carcasses. At Gettysburg,

5,000 horses, mules, and more than 7,000 human bodies littered the land, including farm animals, cattle, oxen, chickens, and sheep. Widowed Lydia Leister, whose small home on Cemetery Ridge became Union General George Meade's headquarters, returned after the battle to her seven acres and found 17 dead horses in her yard near her house. She somehow endured the odor until the dead horses became part of an estimated five million pounds of horseflesh burned on the Gettysburg battlefield. She finally sold the bones of burned horse carcasses to a collector. Burning horse carcasses did not immediately eliminate the horrible odor; it made it worse. After the Battle of Antietam, wounded soldiers had to be removed rapidly from the battlefield because the odor from burning horses could not be tolerated.[203]

It took time for large battlefields to return to typical fields. The battle at Brawner's Farm was fought on August 28th, 1862. Confederates, after the battle, removed the last useable clothing from rotting corpses. Stragglers were then ordered to throw dirt over the bodies in a half-hearted attempt at burial. Over a year later, John Gibbon, one of the Union commanders who fought in the battle, rode over the battlefield and could trace the battle line by the thousands of cartridge papers and partially buried bodies. The latter were easy to find because the grass was greener and taller where men died. The battlefield shocked a soldier from New York who also saw the battlefield a year later and wrote, "The sight was indeed sickening. Lying about in every direction were bleaching bones and ghastly skulls."[204]

Like others, the battlefield at Antietam was disturbing. Private George K. Harlow was part of the Confederate forces on their way to

---

203 Billings, *Hardtack and Coffee*, 106-107. Browning and Silver, *An Environmental History of the Civil War*, 102, 119-120. Hess, *Animal Histories of the Civil War Era*, 60, 76. *Harper's Pictorial History of the Civil War*, 355.
204 Gaff, *Brave Men's Tears*, 178.

Gettysburg when they passed the Antietam battlefield. Curiosity compelled him to visit the battle site, and what he saw traumatized him.

> I have been this morning over the old Sharpsburg battlefield this morning and have witnessed the most horrible sights that my eyes ever beheld I saw dead yankees in any number just lying on top of the ground with little dirt thrown over them and hogs rooting them out of the ground and eating them and others lying on top of the ground with the flesh picked off and their bones bleaching and they by many hundreds! oh what a horrible sight for human beings to look upon in a civilized Country! When will this horrid war ever end; God grant the time may spedily [sic] the time may soon come that piece [sic] may return to our once happy Country and our lives be spare to meet each other again on earth.[205]

If horses and mules could articulate their feelings, they would agree with Private Harlow about ending the war. Although they played a secondary role to the humans who controlled them, war animals played a vital role in the war and paid a heavy price. They were a crucial part of a war that changed America. It was a war where the union was saved by the victory of the industrial North, which defeated an agrarian South, left in ruins, struggling for a century to recover. Four million enslaved people were freed and continued to fight for equality. Among the superior resources of the North that helped win the war were animals, especially horses and cattle.[206]

The magnitude of the changes brought on by the Civil War caused well-known historian Charles A. Beard to call it "the Second American Revolution." The devastation of the war can be seen in

---

[205] John M. Priest, *Antietam: The Soldiers' Battle* (Shippensburg, Pennsylvania: White Mane Publishing, 1989), 316.
[206] Armistead, *Horses and Mules in the Civil War*, 95-102. Worman, *Civil War Animal Heroes*, 65-73, 98-104.

the destruction of property and loss of human and animal life. Confederate soldiers had a one out of four chance of not surviving the war, and the North lost nearly 20 percent of its young men. A future generation was lost. Young women lacked men their age to marry and were forced to remain single or marry older men. The number of domesticated animals declined. The population of hogs declined by 25 percent, and that of horses was devastated by losses of as high as 40 percent in Virginia and 45 percent in Georgia.

Despite the commendable valor of many of the men and women of both combatants during the war, the repulsive and brutal nature of war, which diminishes the value and respect for life, raises the question of how far humankind has really evolved from our primitive ancestors. After all the ordeals of war animals, especially horses, the paramount war animals that suffered half a million more fatalities than humans, they would probably have a query for their human counterparts: "What have you gotten us into?"

BIBLIOGRAPHICAL COMMENT

Materials used in preparing this volume are in the footnotes. The history of animals and the Civil War has been ignored until recently. Much of the information about animals and the Civil War is fragmented and scattered throughout primary sources written by participants in the war and more recent secondary works. About a dozen recent publications have attempted to fill the long-standing gap in the history of animals and war. These do not entirely fill the gap, but they are the start of more attention to the history of animals. Helpful information is available on websites like Wikipedia and the National Park Service. The titles mentioned below were selected because they are generally accessible for further reading.

Most histories of animals and the Civil War concern horses and dogs. Only a few deal with other animals. Two scholarly works—Earl J. Hess' *Animal Histories of the Civil War Era* (2022) and Judkin Browning and Timothy Silver's *An Environmental History of the Civil War* (2020) are among works giving a broader overview. Charles G. Worman's *Civil War Animal Heroes: Mascots, Pets and War Horses* (2011) also provides a more comprehensive range of animals in the war.

An excellent history of horses in America is Ann Norton Greene's *Horses at Work* (2008). Covering their role in the Civil War are *Horses and Mules in the Civil War: A Complete History with a Roster of More Than 700 War Horses* (2013) by Gene C. Armistead and *Horses in Gray: Famous Confederate Warhorses* (2017) by J. D. R. Hawkins. Francis T. Miller's *The Photographic History of the Civil War in Ten Volumes (Volume IV): The Cavalry* (1911) has valuable information. For cavalry tactics and training of Union cavalry, see Philip St. George Cooke's *The 1862 U.S. Cavalry Tactics* (1862). One of the earliest books on horses and the Civil War is the readable *Famous Horses of the Civil War* (1959) by Fairfax Downey, written for young readers. For another early book on horses, consult Sue Cottrell's *Hoof Beats North and South* (1975). For mules, see Emmett M. Essin's *Shavetails & Bell Sharps: The History of the U.S. Army Mule* (1997); Nancy F. McEntee's *Haversacks, Hardtack, and Unserviceable Mules* (2017); and Captain Henry A. Castle's *The Army Mule* (1897). Rebecca Frankel's *War Dogs* (2014) ably covers the history of canines. Other works include Anne Palagruto's *Civil War Dogs and the Men Who Loved Them* (2008) and Marilyn Seguin's *Dogs of War* (1998). One of the better books on dogs is *Loyal Hearts: Histories of American Civil War Canines* (2009) by Michael Zucchero. Thought-provoking is *The Intelligence of Dogs: Canine Consciousness and Capabilities* by psychologist Stanley Coren.

The history of disease and medical treatment is covered in Paul E. Steiner's *Disease in the Civil War* (1968), Walter R. Heiss' *Veterinary Service During the American Civil War* (2005), Stewart Brooks' *Civil War Medicine* (1966), George W. Adams' *Doctors in Blue* (1985), H. H. Cunningham's *Doctors in Gray* (1970), and Susan P. Beller's *Medical Practices in the Civil War* (1992).

Former Union soldier John D. Billings' *Hardtack and Coffee* (1888) expertly describes the life of the Civil War soldier and provides information about animals. A Confederate veteran, Alexander Hunter, also provides useful information in *Johnny Reb and Billy Yank* (1904). More recent accounts by Bell I. Wiley include *The Life of Johnny Reb* (1943), *The Life of Billy Yank* (1952), *The Common Soldier of the Civil War* (1943), and James I. Robertson, Jr.'s *Soldiers Blue and Gray* (1988).

Edward Boykin's *Beefsteak Raid* (1960) covers the story of Confederates raiding and stealing approximately 3,000 cattle from the Union in 1864. Hunger in Civil War prisons is discussed in Roger Pickenpaugh's *Captives in Gray* (2009), William B. Hesseltine's *Civil War Prisons* (1930), J. Osborn Coburn's *Hell on Belle Isle* (1997), Ovid L. Futch's *History of Andersonville Prison* (2011), and George Levy's *To Die in Chicago* (1999).

John L. Heatwole's *The Burning: Sheridan's Devastation of the Shenandoah Valley* (1998) covers the Union burning the Shenandoah Valley under Sheridan, as does Michael G. Mahon's *The Shenandoah Valley* (1999), Jack H. Lepa's *The Shenandoah Valley Campaign of 1864* (2003), Gary W. Gallagher's *Struggle for the Shenandoah* (1991), and Ray A. Neff's *Valley of the Shadow* (1987). The torching of Loudoun Valley is discussed in *From Frontier to Suburbia* (2005) by Charles P. Poland, Jr. For Sherman's destruction of Georgia and the Carolinas in 1864, see Joseph T. Glatthaar's *The March to the Sea and Beyond* (1985), Richard Wheeler's *Sherman's March* (1978), and B. H. Liddell Hart's *Sherman* (1993).

The weaponry of the war is presented in detail in *Confederate Edged Weapons* (1960) by William A. Albaugh III, *Civil War Guns* (1962) by William B. Edwards, *Weapons of the American Civil War* (1987) by Ian V. Hogg, *Civil War Projectiles II: Small Arms & Field*

Artillery (1980) by W. Reid McKee and M. E. Mason, Jr., and *Cannons* (1985) by Dean Thomas.

For the beneficial impact that animals can have on improving human life, see "Walk a Hound: dog walking and the wellbeing of older adults" by Lynette P. Harvey in *Educational Gerontology*, 2024, vol. 50, no. 7, 594-608.

The work of the Livestock Conservancy to save endangered breeds of horses, asses, sheep, goats, rabbits, pigs, and poultry are succinctly discussed in "The Livestock Conservancy on Wikipedia.

John W Busey's, *These Honored Dead* (1988), Drew G. Faust's *Republic of Suffering* (2008), Mary H. Mitchell's *Hollywood Cemetery* (1985) and Steven Stotelmyer's *The Bivouacs of the Dead* (1992) tell about the sorrowful burial of the Civil War dead.

INDEX

Note: Page numbers in *italic* figures and page numbers followed by "n" refer to notes.

Ajax (horse), 69
Alentharpe, W., 81
alligator, 106, 113
American cavalry, 9
American Civil war. *See* Civil War
American revolution, 9
ancient world warfare, 8
Andersonville Civil War Prison (Davis), 118
Andersonville Prison, 117, *119*
Andrews, Eliza, 146
animals as military targets, 138. See also war animals' struggle; warfare animals
burning of Shenandoah valley, 139–42
destruction of Georgia, 144–47
destruction of Loudoun Valley, 142–44
marching through Carolinas, 147–50
Sherman's March, 144–50
"swamp ranging", 148
targeting Southern livestock and resources, 138–39
Union strategy of total war, 138–39
animals' intelligence, 96

animal-human bond. *See* human-animal bond
animal suicide, 173
Antietam, Battle of (1862), 86, 180–81
bees attack during, 115
need of care for wounded men at, 166
temporary Union hospital after, *167*
von Bachelle's dog at, 165
wounds of horses at, 75
Antietam Campaign, 56, 72
anti-tank dogs, 23–24, 24n31
ants, 109
Appomattox Campaign, 69, 96
Armistead, Gene C., 68
arms and ammunition, 65–66
artillery horses, 163, *164*
Ashby, Turner, 74, 76–77, *77*
Atlanta Campaign, raid in, 61, 62
Attila the Hun, 13

baboon, 20–21
badger, 106
Bainbridge, David, 45
Baldwin, William, 80
Baldy (horse), 74, 75, *75*, 90
Ball's Bluff, Battle of (1861), 120
"barking dog regiment". *See* 104th Ohio Infantry
Bastet, 17
bat bomb project, 24
Bate, William B., 98
bats, 24
battlefield remains, 120–21
bayonets, 67
Beard, Charles A., 181
bears, 106, 113, 116
Beauregard, General, 155
bed bugs, 108, 109
beef, 122–28, 129–30, 131–34
"Beefsteak Raid" (1864), 125, *126*

bees, 15, 108, 113, 115–16
Big Sorrel (horse), 71
Billings, John D., 84, 86, 87, 109, 130, 133, 163
Billy (horse), 79
Billy Yank (Union soldiers), 132
birds, 4, 14, 20, 162
Black Bess (mare), 98
Blackford, William, 91, 97
Black Hawk (stallion), 98
blacksnakes, 106
bloodletting, 69
Blue Peacock project, 22, 23, 23n29
Bomber (cat), 18n18
Brandy Station, Battle of, 57, 60n65
Brawner's Farm, battle at, 115, 162, 180
Bronze Age, 8
Brown-roan. See The Roan
Buell, Don Carlos, 152
bulldog, 101, 116
Bull Run, Battle of:
first, 36, 75, 75n78, 120, 155, 158
second, 69, 115, 162
bulls, 22
bumblebees, 115
bummers, 145, 147–50
Burden, Henry, 45
burial practices, 173
Andersonville cemetery, *176*
after Battle of Fair Oaks, *178*
burial process, 173–74
burial trenches, 176
burning of horse carcasses, *178*
of Confederate dead, *175*, 177
dead on Gettysburg battlefield, *174*
movement by Southern Memorial Association, 177
sickness and struggles of, *179*
"The Burning". See Shenandoah Valley, burning of
Burns (horse), 90–91

Burnside, Ambrose, 57, 154, 160
"Burnst Country", 146
Burrows, J. L., 116
Butler, Benjamin, 91
buzzard, 106

camel, 12–13
  Arabian, 92
  Bactrian, 92
  caravans, 92
  cavalry, 13, 13n10
  import from Africa and Middle East, 92
  Jefferson Davis's desert experiment, 91–93
  Old Douglas, 107
  rebellious nature of, 91–93
Camp Douglas, 135, 136
Camp Verde, 92
canaries, 20
canines. *See* dog
canine therapy, 172
cat, 16–18, 23, 106
  Bomber, 18n18
  as food, 123
cattles, 4, 122, 125–26, 128–30
cavalry. *See also* Confederate cavalry; Union cavalry
  American cavalry, 9
  camel, 13, 13n10
  'Cow Cavalry', 129
  depot, 37n45, 38, *39*
  horse, 8, 9
  "Kil-Cavalry", 58
  Lydian cavalry, 13
  moose cavalry, 16, 16n16
  Persian cavalry, 13
  shoeing cavalry horse, *46*
  Cavalry Bureau (1863), 29, 37, 38
  cavalry training, 50
  care of cavalry horses, 53
  cavalry tactics in, 62–67

Confederate cavalry, 56–62
evolution of weapons, 62–67
foot soldiers and cavalrymen, 55–56
manuals and battlefield experience, 51–52
Union cavalry camps, 53
Union cavalry recruits, 53–55
Union *vs.* Confederate advantage, 52
Cedar Creek, Battle of (1864), 67, 78, 139
Chamberlain, Joshua L., 79
Chambersburg Raid (1864), 60, 62, 139
Chambliss, John R., 48, 58–59
chameleon, 106
Chancellorsville, Battle of (1863), 61, 125
Charlemagne (horse), 79
Charley (horse), 89
Charlie (dog), 165
Cheat Mountain combat (1861), 113
chickens, 4, 20, 22, 106
chiggers, 108, 109
Chimborazo Hospital in Richmond, war at, 168
Cincinnati (horse), 74, *74*
Civil War (1861–1865), 4–6, 9, 25–26
animals' role and sacrifice, 4–6
backbone of Civil War's mobility, 26–27
battles and military actions, 162
care of mounts, 36–49
Cavalry Bureau, 37
Confederate struggle with financing and tax, 33
corrals at Giesboro, *40*
diseases causing death, 153
dismount camp, 38
equine warriors in, 26–27
evolution of weapons and cavalry tactics, 62–67
farriers at Giesboro, *47*
food shortages, 153–57
Forrest and Mosby's impact, 60–61
Giesboro cavalry depot, 37n45, 38, *39*
horse infirmaries, 41
horse racing in maintaining morale, 81–82

horse-related injuries and casualties, 79–81
impressment prices, *32*
legendary horses of, 68–79
loyalty of war horses during, 98–99
mascots, 105–7
McClellan saddle, 48–49
medical challenges during, 152–53
obtaining horses and mules, 28–36
principal commanders of, 94
prison conditions, 108–9, 112, 116–19, *119*, 135–37
produce loans, 33–34
property seizure form, *31*
remount stations, 38
role and treatment of animals, 94–96
shoeing cavalry horse, *46*
shoeing mule, *48*
strain of inflation and horse losses, 34–35
struggle for cavalry, 36–49
struggle for mules, 35–36
Union cavalry depots, 38–40
Union hay wharf, *43*
Civil War, Spanish (1930s), 20
Cleburne, Patrick, 113
Clune, Frank, 81
Clydesdales, 52
Coburn, J. Osborn, 136
"coffee coolers", 38
Coffin, Charles Carleton, 36
Columbia, burning of, 149
combat fatigue. *See* Da Costa's syndrome
Comet (horse), 91, 97
Confederacy, *127*
"Beefsteak Raid", 125, *126*
cattle supply efforts in Florida, 128–29
horse infirmaries, 41
impressment of horses and mules, 28–31
impressment prices, *32*
occupation in Centreville, 120, 159
property seizure form, *31*

Confederate cavalry, 56
fall of Vicksburg, 58
Forrest and Mosby's impact, 60–61
Gettysburg campaign and decline of, 57, 58
horse shortages, 58–59
"Mosby's Confederacy", 61
roles and impact of cavalry raids, 61–62
struggles with resources, 58–59
successful encounters of, 60
Confederates, 151
Camp Verde capture by, 92
food shortages, 123, 155–56
hunting and slaughtering rabbits, 124
losses during retreat after Battle of Franklin, 36
official rations for, 122–23
Pickett's Charge, 64, 165
problems in providing beef as rations, 131
resource destruction, 143–44
struggle with financing and tax, 33
visits to Manassas battlefield, 120
women suffering, 149–50
Continental Army, 9
Cooke, Philip St. George, 52
Corcoran, Michael, 80
Coren, Stanley, 96
Corinth, Battle of, 105
Corporal Jackie (baboon), 21, 21n25
corrals at Giesboro, *40*
cow, 95
'Cow Cavalry', 128–29
Crimean War, 49
crow, 106, 120
Cryptochrome (Cry4), 14n12
Culp's Hill, Battle of (1863), 103
Culp's Hill dog, 103
Curly (dog), 165
Cushing, A. H., 165–66
Custer, George A., *101*

Cyrus the Great of Persia, 13

Da Costa's syndrome, 172
Dandy (horse), 79
Daniel Webster (horse), 79
Davis, Captain, 89
Davis, Jefferson, 34, 36, 69, 91–93, 135, 155
Davis, Robert S., 118
dead, disrupters of, 120–21
deer, 4, 112
Defense Advanced Research Projects Agency (DARPA), 18
Dick (sheep), 124
diets, desperation, 134–37
dismount camp, 38
dog (canines), 4, 13–14, 14n11, 23–24, 95–96, 106
canine therapy, 172
captured Confederate dog, *101*
Charlie, 165
companions, 95, 99–104
Culp's Hill dog, 103
Curly, 165
as food, 134–35, 135–36
Grace, 103
guard, 108
Hero, 116, *117*
intelligence, 96
Jack, 101, *102*
Jack Russell terrier, 100
killing by bummers, 147–48
Newfoundland, 95, 100, 165
104th Ohio Infantry, 100
prison dogs, 116–19
protecting dead owner's body, *103*
Russian bloodhound, 116
Sallie, 101, 103, 165
St. Bernard, 103
treatment in Civil war, 95
wounds, 164–66
dolphins, 18

INDEX

donkey, 10, 10n6, 25
Douglas, Henry Kyd, 143, 160
draft horse, 52
Dranesville, Battle of, 159
Drimeyer, Henry, 81
dromedary camel (Old Douglas), 107

eagles, 105–7
Early, Jubal, 139
Ebony (horse), 91
elephants, 11, 11n8
English Carrier pigeons, 14n13
equine(s), 26–27, 50
human-equine bond, 97–99
rehabilitation depots, 153

Fair Oaks, Battle of (1862), 82, 178
Fancy (horse), 68, 71–73, *73*, 73n76, 80, 90
Farnsworth, Elon John, 57, 58
farriers at Giesboro, *47*
Ferguson, John, 104
"Fighting Billy". *See* Bate, William B.
"Fighting Joe" Wheeler. *See* Wheeler, Joseph
"Fighting Joe Hooker". *See* Hooker, Joe
Fire-eater (horse), 79
Fisher's Hill, Battle of (1864), 139
fleas, 111–12
flies, 109, 120
Florida's cow cavalry, 128–29
foods, survival, 122
beef, 122–28, 128–30, 131–34
Beefsteak Raid, 125, *126*, 129n152
cattle logistics and butchery, 129–30
challenges in rations and preservation, 131–34
desperation diets, 134–37
feeding and economies, 122–28
Florida's cow cavalry, 128–29
food in prisons, 134–37

hardtack, 132, *133*
hippophagy, 135
steers, 129, *130*, *131*
United States Army regulations, 122
foragers, 145
foraging Confederate resources, 144–47
foraging conflict in Dranesville, 120
Forrest, Nathan Bedford, 60, 79–80, 88, 97, 98
"41 Tactics". *See* Poinsett's Tactics
foxes, 106
Francis, Tim, 16
Franklin, Battle of (1864), 36
Fredericksburg, Battle of (1862), 104, 160
Frémont, General, 154

Gaines' Mill, Battle of (1862), 103
geese, 106, 145
Georgia destruction, 144–47
German Shepherds, 23
Gettysburg, Battle of (1863), 58
burial of dead, *174*, *175*
Pickett's Charge, 64, 165
Gettysburg Campaign (1863), 27, 57
Gettysburg National Cemetery, 177
Gibbon, John, 180
Giesboro:
cavalry depot, 37n45, 38, *39*
corrals at, *40*
farriers at, *47*
Gilmer, Harry, 141
gnats, 108, 112
goats, 5
Gonatas, Antigonus II, 21
Gordon, John Brown, 166
Grace (mongrel), 103
"granary of the South" destruction, 149
Grant, Ulysses S., 63, 74, 80, 89, 94, 139–40, 147, 158, 164
graybacks. *See* lice

INDEX

Greenbrier. *See* Traveller
Grierson, Benjamin, 58, 61–62
Grimes, Bryan, 103
guard dogs, 108
Gulf Wars, 20

Halleck, General, 37
Hampton, Wade, 60, 87, 125, 147
Hancock, Winfield Scott, 163
Hannibal, general, 11, 11n8, 22
hardtack, 132, *133*
Hardtack and Coffee (Billings), 109, *133*
Harlow, George K., 180–81
Harpers Ferry, war at, 71, 80, 81, 86
Hatcher's Run, Battle of (1865), 165
Hatra, Siege of (198 BC), 16
Hawkins, J. D. R., 72
Hero (dog), 116, *117*
HerorATs, 19n21
hinny, 10n6
hippophagy, 135
hogs, 4, 123
homing pigeon, 14–15, 15n14
Hood, John B., 35
Hooker, Joe, 154, 161
hornets, 115
horse(s), 4, 7, 8–10, 9n1, 9n2, 9n3, 10n4, 10n5, 25n33, 50. *See also* mule(s)
Ajax, 69
artillery horses, 163, *164*
Baldy, 74, 75, *75*, 90
Big Sorrel, 71
Billy, 79
Black Bess, 98
Black Hawk, 98
Burns, 90–91
cavalry, 8, 9
Charlemagne, 79

Charley, 89
Cincinnati, 74, *74*
in Civil war, 25, 26, 28
combat behaviour, 163
Comet, 91, 97
Dandy, 79
dangers of horsemanship, 79–81
Daniel Webster, 79
desirable Union officer's mount, *83*
disease and death, 151–53
draft horse, 52
Ebony, 91
equine rehabilitation depots, 153
Fancy, 68, 71–73, *73*, 73n76, 80, 90
Fire-eater, 79
as food, 135
horseshoes, 44–45
injuries and casualties, 79–81
Jeff Davis, 74, *74*
Kangaroo, 89
killings by bummers, 148–49
King Philip, 79
legendary Civil War, 68–79
Lexington, 79
loyalty of war horses, 97–99
Lucy Long, 69
Maud, 99
vs. mule, 85
obtaining horses for military, 28–36
onchocerciasis, 112
Quarter Horses, 82
racehorses, 81–82
rebellious nature of, 89–91
Richmond, 69
Rienzi, 74, 78–79, *78*
The Roan, 69
Roderick, 79, 97
Sam, 79
shoeing cavalry horse, *46*

"shoeless", 44
sitting like dog, *90*
Standardbreds, 82
Thoroughbreds, 82
Tom Telegraph, 74, 76–77,
training, 8, 50–51
Traveller, 68, 70–71, *71*, 74, 80
type and size of, 7
wounds, 163, 171
horseflies, 111
horseshoes, 44–45
Hough, Brian, 19
hound(s), 100, 116, 118
human-animal bond, 94, 151
bond with equines, 97–99
canine companions, 95, 99–104
fondness for animals, 94–95
loyalty of war horses, 97–99
mascots and pets, 105–7
role and treatment of animals, 94–96
Hunter, Alexander, 99, 156, 167–68

insect(s), 4, 120, 172
ants, 109
bees, 15, 108, 113, 115–16
hornets, 115
incessant bites of, 108
mosquito, 15, 108, 112
tormentors, 109–13
The Intelligence of Dogs: Canine Consciousness and Capabilities (Coren), 96
intestinal worms, 108
I Rode with Stonewall (Douglas), 160

Jack (Bulldog or Bull Terrier), 101, *102*
Jack Russell terrier, 100
Jackson, Anna, 90
Jackson, Stonewall, 68, 71, 72, 76, 80, 90, 100, 115, 159, 160
Jeff Davis (horse), 74, *74*

Johnny Reb (Confederate soldiers), 132
Johnson, Andrew, 35
Johnston, Albert Sidney, 79
Jomini, Antoine-Henri, 63

Kadesh, Battle of (1274 BC), 20–21
Kane, Thomas L., 103
Kangaroo (horse), 89
Kees, John, 157
Kentucky Campaign (1862), 154
Kernstown, second Battle of (1864), 139
"Kil-Cavalry", 58
Kilpatrick-Dahlgren raid, 58
Kilpatrick, Hugh Judson, 57, 58
King Cotton diplomacy, 26
King Philip (horse), 79
Korean War, 19

lambs, 106
Larson, C. Kay, 25
Lawson, Thomas, 152
Lee, Custis, 70
Lee, Robert E., 57, 58, 61, *71*, 96, 123, 147
fondness for animals, 94–95
horses, 68–71
injury, 80
and Mud March, 160
reconnaissance mission with camels and mules, 93
suffering of infantry, 139, 149–50, 156–57
Lee, Robert E. Jr., 69
Leister, Lydia, 180
Lexington (horse), 79
lice, 108, 109, 112
boiling clothes, *111*
picking lice off from clothing, 109, *110*
"Lige" White, 141
Lightning Mule Brigade, 87
Lincoln, Abraham, 125, 154, 161, 177

pragmatic view on generals and horses, 56
runaway horse incident, 91
troop review, 91
Lincoln, William, 100
lion, 20, 21
Little Sorrel. *See* Fancy (horse)
livestock. *See* cattles
lizards, 114
Long Drive (1866–1888), 128
Lord, Margaret, 114
Loudoun Valley destruction (1864), 142–44
Lucy Long (horse), 69
Lunt, Dolly, 145
Lydian cavalry, 13

M1855 rifle-musket, *64*
maggots, 109, 120, 132
magnetoreception, 14
Mahon, Michael, 144
mail pigeons. *See* homing pigeon
malaria outbreak in Union Army, 112
Manassas, Battle of. *See* Bull Run, Battle of
March to the Sea (Sherman's campaign), 155
mascots, 5, 105–7
alligator, 106
badger, 106
canines as, 95
crow, 106
Dick, 124
eagles, 106
Jack, 101
Jackie, 21
Jack Russell terrier mascot, 100
Old Douglas, 107
pelican, 106
Sallie, 101–3, 165
wildcat, 106
Maud (horse), 99

McClellan, George B., 37, 48–49, 49n56, 56, 61, 79, 90, 91, 158
Meade, George, 74, 75, 90, 180
Meagher, Thomas F., 82
Megara, Siege of (266 BC), 21
Meigs, John Rodgers, 140
Meigs, Montgomery, 28, 29, 30n36, 42, 57
Merritt, Wesley, 141
messenger pigeons. *See* homing pigeon
Mexican mustang, 84
mice, baby, 106
Middle Ages, 8
Miller, C. S., 81
Miller, John, 81
Milton, John, 31
Mine Run Campaign (1863), 154
Minié ball, 62
Mississippi River control (1863), 126, 138–39
mites, 108, 109, 112
monkeys, 21
Montgomery, J. R., 171–72
moose, 16
moose cavalry, 16, 16n16
Morgan, John Hunt, 62, 98
Mosby, John S., 55, 60–61, 66, 79, 138, 141
attack on Union supply train, 115
raid at Fairfax Courthouse, 56
raids and guerrilla activity in Shenandoah Valley, 138
Rangers formation, 55
Mosgrove, George Dallas, 124, 125
mosquitoes, 15, 108, 112
Mother Bickerdyke, 109
Mud March (1863), 160–61, *161*
mule(s), 4, 10–11, 10n6, 11n7, 25, 27, 50. *See also* horses
disease and death, 151–53
equine rehabilitation depots, 153
as food, 135
vs. horse, 85
killing by bummers, 148–49

Lighting Mule Brigade, 87
mule-producing state for Union, 84
obtaining mules for military, 28–36
pack mule, *51*
perils in treacherous terrain, 88–89, *88*
pole mules, 85
rebellious nature of, 84–89
shoeing mule, *48*
six mule team, *86*
swing mules, 85
training challenges for, 50–51
Murfreesboro, Battle of, 162
muskrat, 123
Myers, A. C., 34, 36

Napoleon, 12
Napoleonic wars, 8
Naval Marine Mammal Program, 18
Newfoundlanders (dog), 95, 100, 165
New Market, Battle of (1864), 100
Nisbet, James C., 149
"The North's Andersonville", 135

Old Abe (Bald eagle), 105, *106*, 105n122
Old Douglas (camel), 107
Old Fancy. *See* Fancy (horse)
Old Sorrel. *See* Fancy (horse)
onchocerciasis, 112
104th Ohio Infantry, 100
"Operation Kuwaiti Field Chicken", 20
opossum, 118
Ouchley, Kelby, 124
ox, 4, 12, 12n9, 22

pack mule, *51*
pelican, 106
Pelusium, Battle of (525 BC), 17
Pember, Phoebe Yates, 119, 168–169

Peninsular Campaign (1862), 95, 158–159
Percherons, 52
Perryville, Battle of (1862), 156–57
Persian cavalry, 13
Petersburg Campaign, 75, 89, 100, 125
Pfieff, Louis, 104
Pickett Charge, 64, 165
Pickett, General, 64
Pierce, Franklin, 91
pigeons, 22. *See also* homing pigeon
pigs, 19–20, 21, 106
"War Pig", 20n22, 21n26
Pleasonton, Alfred, 61
Poinsett, J. R., 52
"Poinsett's Tactics", 51–52
pole mules, 85
Polley, J. B., 56
pork, 122, 132
Port Republic, Battle of (1862), 87
Price, Sterling, 60
prison dogs, 116–18
prisoner-of-war camps, 135–37
produce loans, 33–34
"Project Acoustic Kitty", 17, 18n18
Project Pigeon, 22
PTSD (post-traumatic stress disorder), 172
Pyrrhus, Greek king, 20

quail, 125
Quakers, 141–42
Quantrill, William Clarke, 89
Quarter Horses, 82

rabbits, 4, 144
slaughter in east Tennessee, 124–25
raccoons, 106
racehorses, 81–82
Ramesses II, 20

ramrod, 65
Ramsdell, Charles W., 32
rats, 18–19, 19n21
  as food, 135
Recollections of Libby Prison (Burrows), 116
reindeer, 16, 16n17
remount depots (1863), 38–39
Rhodes, Charles D., 42, 44, 52
Rhodes, Elisha Hunt, 124
Richmond (horse), 69
Rienzi (horse), 74, 78–79, *78*
rifle-musket, 63, *63*–64
The Roan (horse), 69
Roderick (horse), 79, 97
Roman poisoning with honey (69 BC), 15
Romney Expedition, 159–60
rooster, 107
roundworms, 113
Russell, William H., 36
Russian bloodhound, 116

sabers, 67
saddle tree, 48
Sallie (bull terrier), 101, 103, 165
Sam (horse), 79
scabies, 108
Schurz, Carl, 154
Scipio Africanus, 11
scorpions, 16
Scott, Winfield, 36, 163
sea lions, 18
seals, 18
"Second American Revolution" (Civil War), 181–82
Second Punic War, 22
Seven Days' Battles, 69
seven-shot Spencer rifle, 66
Shannon, Fred A., 29
sheep, 4, 95

Dick, 124
shell shock. *See* Da Costa's syndrome
Shenandoah Campaign (1864), 67
The Shenandoah Valley (Mahon), 144
Shenandoah Valley, burning of (1864), 139–44
Sheridan, Philip, 60, 66, 74, 77, 79, 139, 140–44
Sherman, Charles, 81
Sherman, William Tecumseh, 35, 60, 79, 95, 140–44
marching through Carolinas, 147–50
March to the Sea, 144–47
"Sherman Neckties", 147
Shiloh, Battle of (1862), 98, 104, 158, 164
shoeing:
cavalry horse, 46
mule, 48
skunks, 108, 113
smoothbore musket, 62–63
snakes, 108, 113–14
"The Snapping Turtle". *See* Baldy
Song Dynasty, 21–22
"soldier's heart". *See* Da Costa's syndrome
soldiers' struggles, 151
burial of dead, 173–82, *174*, *175*
casualties of war, 173–82
combat, 162
disease and death, 151–53
hunger, 153–57
psychological toll of war, 172–73
"sun struck", 158
weather impact, 157–61
wounds, 163–71
Sorrel, Little/Old. *See* Fancy (horse)
Soviet moose cavalry experiment (1939–1940), 16
"sowbelly", 132
Spanish Civil War (1930s), 20
sparrows, 162
Spessard, Captain, 166
Spotsylvania, Battle of (1864), 70

squirrels, 125
Standardbreds, 82
Stanton, Edwin M., 35, 55
St. Bernard (dog), 103
steers, 129, *130*, *131*
Stoneman, George, 61
Stoughton, Edwin, 56
Streight, Abel D., 87
Stuart, Jeb, 56–57, 60, 61, 62, 69, 91, 159
suicide-like behaviors in animals, 173
Suttle, Danael Christian, 82
"swamp ranging", 148
swing mules, 85

tapeworms, 113
Tarsier, 173
"teeth duller". *See* hardtack
Tensdale, George A., 81
Themiscyra, defense of (72 BC), 15
Thomas, George H., 79
Thoroughbreds, 82
Thymbra, Battle of, 13
Tian Dan, 22
ticks, 111, 112, 128
Tom Telegraph (horse), 74, 76–77
tormentors, 108
alligators, 113
ants, 109
battlefield remains and disruptions, 120–21
bed bugs, 108, 109
bees, 108, 113, 115–16
chiggers, 108, 109
crows, 120
disrupters of dead, 120–21
fleas, 111–12
flies, 109, 120
gnats, 108, 112
guard dogs, 108

insects, 109–13
intestinal worms, 108
lice, 108, 109–11, 112
lizards, 114
maggots, 109, 120
mites, 108, 109, 112
mosquitos, 108, 112
parasites, 109–13
prison dogs, 116–18
rats, 119
reptiles, 113–14
roundworms, 113
scabies, 108
skunks, 108, 113
snakes, 108, 113–14
suffering of soldiers and animals, 108–9
tapeworms, 113
ticks, 111, 112
Traveller (horse), 68, 70–71, *71*, 74, 80, 94–95
Trevilian Station, Battle of, 60, 60n65
Tunnard, Willie, 170
turkeys, 20
Turner, Edward, 118

Union Army, 28, 151
capture of Fort Henry, 158
capture of Vicksburg, 126, 138–39
capturing Camp Verde, 92
cattle logistics and butchery, 129–30
cook, *134*
impressment of horses, 28–30
Lighting Mule Brigade, 87
malaria outbreak in, 112
Mississippi River control, 126, 138–39
official rations for, 122
prisoner-of-war camp, 135–36
problems in providing beef as rations, 131
retreat, 161
strategy of total war, 138–39

Union hay wharf, *43*
Union cavalry, 57–58
camps, 53
depots, 38–40
recruits, 53–55
United States Civil War. *See* Civil War
"Unsinkable Sam", 18, 18n19

Valley Campaign (1862), 154
Valverde, Battle of (1862), 157
Vanderbilt, George, 53
veterinarian medicine, 153
Vicksburg, Battle of, 58, 61, 112, 114, 135, 158, 170
Vicksburg Campaign, 61, 80, 107
Vicksburg, Siege of, 114, 135, 158, 170
Vietnam war, 14
Virginia Military Institute (VMI), 72
Von Bachelle, Werner, 165

war animals' struggle, 151
burial of dead, 178–82
disease and death, 151–53
forgotten casualties of war, 178–82
hunger, 153–57
psychological toll of war, 172–73
impact of warfare on, 162
weather impact, 157–61
wounds, 163–71
warfare animals, 4, 7
baboon, 20, 21
bees, 15
bulls, 22
camel, 12–13
canaries, 20
cats, 16–18, 23
chickens, 20, 22
dog, 4, 13–14, 23–24
dolphins, 18
donkeys, 10, 11

elephants, 11, 11n8
horses, 4, 7–10
humans and, 5
lion, 20, 21
monkeys, 21
moose, 16
mosquitoes, 15
mule, 10–11
oxen, 12, 22
pigeons, 14–15, 15n14, 22
rats, 18–19
reindeer, 16
scorpions, 16
sea lions, 18
seals, 18
strategic use of, 15–21
suicide missions, 21–24
pigs, 19–20, 21
turkeys, 20
"War Pig", 20n22, 21n26
War Pigeons, 15n14
wasps, 115
Wauhatchie, Battle of (1863), 87
weapons, 62
arms and ammunition, 65–66
M1855 rifle-musket, *64*
Minié ball, 62, *63*
ramrod, *65*
rifle-musket, *63*, 63–64
sabers and bayonets, 67
seven-shot Spencer rifle, 66
smoothbore musket, 62–63
Webster, Frederick, 73n76
weevils, 132
Wheeler, Joseph, 62, 147
wildcat, 106
Wilderness, Battle of the (1864), 167, 170
wounded trapped in fire during, *170*
Williams, General, 147

Wilson, James H., 35
Wilson's Creek, Battle of (1861), 82
Winchester, Battle of (1864), 67, 139
Wirz, Henry, 117–18
World War I, 9, 15
  cats, 17
  Corporal Jackie, 21
  rats, 19
World War II, 9, 11, 15
  anti-tank dogs project, 23
  bat bomb project, 24
  cats, 16, 17, 18
  dogs, 13
  Project Pigeon, 22
"worm castles", 132
"wrist breakers", 53

yellow jackets, 115
Yellow Tavern, Battle of, 60

Zama, Battle of, 11
Zucchero, Michael, 164